OCCASIONAL PAPER 223

Monetary Union Among Member Countries of the Gulf Cooperation Council

By a Staff Team led by Ugo Fasano

with Andrea Schaechter, Rina Bhattacharya,
Ibrahim Al Gelaiqah, Behrouz Guerami,
Shehadah Hussein, Bright Okogu,
Van Can Thai, and John Wilson

INTERNATIONAL MONETARY FUND
Washington DC
2003

© 2003 International Monetary Fund

Production: IMF Multimedia Services Division
Figures: Martina Vortmeyer
Typesetting: Alicia Etchebarne-Bourdin

Cataloging-in-Publication Data

Monetary union among member countries of the Gulf Cooperation Council/by a
staff team led by Ugo Fasano—Washington, D.C.: International Monetary
Fund, 2003.

    p. cm.—(Occasional paper, 0251-6365; 223)

      Includes bibliographical references.
      ISBN 1-58906-219-1

  1. Gulf Cooperation Council. 2. Monetary union—Persian Gulf Region. 3.
Persian Gulf Region—Economic integration. I. Fasano, Ugo. II. International
Monetary Fund. III. Occasional paper (International Monetary Fund); no. 223
HG3868.55.M67 2003

Price: US$25.00
(US$22.00 to full-time faculty members and
students at universities and colleges)

Please send orders to:
International Monetary Fund, Publication Services
700 19th Street, N.W., Washington, D.C. 20431, U.S.A.
Tel.: (202) 623-7430   Telefax: (202) 623-7201
E-mail: publications@imf.org
Internet: http://www.imf.org

recycled paper

Contents

The following symbols have been used throughout this paper:

. . . to indicate that data are not available;

— to indicate that the figure is zero or less than half the final digit shown, or that the item does not exist;

– between years or months (e.g., 2001–02 or January–June) to indicate the years or months covered, including the beginning and ending years or months;

/ between years (e.g., 2001/02) to indicate a fiscal (financial) year.

"n.a." means not applicable.

"Billion" means a thousand million.

Minor discrepancies between constituent figures and totals are due to rounding.

The term "country," as used in this paper, does not in all cases refer to a territorial entity that is a state as understood by international law and practice; the term also covers some territorial entities that are not states, but for which statistical data are maintained and provided internationally on a separate and independent basis.

Foreword

Member countries of the Cooperation Council for the Arab States of the Gulf (GCC)—Bahrain, Kuwait, Oman, Qatar, Saudi Arabia, and the United Arab Emirates—are embarking on a challenging task: the creation of a monetary union by the end of the current decade. This is a welcome decision that will consolidate their economic integration efforts initiated in the early 1980s. A monetary union will likely expand markets and help promote competitiveness and economic diversification, thus facilitating integration with the global economy. At the same time, it could contribute, together with the broad structural reforms under way, to achieving a common objective of fostering growth and diversification while maintaining macroeconomic stability. It is hoped that closer economic and monetary integration among the GCC countries could also become a catalyst for broader economic cooperation among Middle Eastern countries.

In seeking to achieve full economic integration, the GCC countries will need to address a number of challenges—principally fiscal convergence, establishment of common institutions, and strengthened data quality. The experiences of other monetary unions, particularly in the euro area, suggest that concerted steps should also be taken to ensure an orderly transition toward convergence of policies and targets. GCC countries are already proceeding with policy coordination—collectively pegging the exchange rate to the U.S. dollar and establishing a single common external tariff. However, setting fiscal convergence criteria, especially on fiscal deficits and debt levels, will be a complex task in light of the importance of oil revenue in the GCC countries' budgets and the volatility of oil prices.

Above all, a successful monetary union also requires a strong political commitment among its member countries, as members cede a part of their sovereignty in the economic decision-making process. In addition, a centralized monetary policy within a decentralized fiscal system requires strict adherence to fiscal convergence and greater flexibility in labor and product markets. In this regard, accelerating domestic structural reforms in the individual countries could facilitate the process of integration and enhance its ultimate success. To the countries of the GCC area: you have our best wishes and our commitment to help in any way we can.

George T. Abed
Director
Middle Eastern Department

Preface

The GCC countries decided at the end of 2001 to create a monetary union by 2010. These countries have already made important progress toward economic and financial integration since efforts started in the early 1980s, including the recent adoption of a unified common external tariff. Further progress toward efficient integration and the creation of a monetary union will likely strengthen the environment for non-oil economic growth and create employment opportunities for a rapidly growing national labor force—two important challenges facing GCC countries. However, important steps lie ahead on the way to establish a common currency. This Occasional Paper examines these steps, such as a common code of fiscal conduct, institutional requirements, and structural policies, needed for a successful monetary union among the GCC countries.

The Occasional Paper is the product of a team effort coordinated by Ugo Fasano of the Middle Eastern Department. The main authors are Ugo Fasano and Andrea Schaechter (Monetary and Financial Systems Department). Rina Bhattacharya, Ibrahim Al Gelaiqah, Behrouz Guerami, Shehadah Hussein, Bright Okogu, Van Can Thai, and John Wilson (all of the Middle Eastern Department at the time the paper was prepared) contributed to the appendixes. The authors are grateful to Zubair Iqbal for his guidance and support, and to a number of other colleagues from various departments in the IMF—in particular George T. Abed, Lorenzo Perez, David Burton, Pierre Dhonte, Paul Chabrier, Jean Le Dem, George Tsibouris, Shigeo Kashiwagi, Patricia Brenner, and Hamid Davoodi—for comments received at various stages of the paper. They would also like to thank Behrouz Guerami and Binta Terrier for excellent research assistance, and Esha Ray of the External Relations Department for editing the paper and coordinating its publication.

The opinions expressed in the paper are those of the authors and do not necessarily represent the views of the national authorities, the IMF, or IMF Executive Directors.

Abbreviations and Acronyms

AML	Anti-money laundering
CPI	Consumer price index
BEAC	Banque des États de l'Afrique Centrale
BCEAO	Banque Centrale des États de l'Afrique de l'Ouest
BMA	Bahrain Monetary Agency
CAEMC	Central African Economic and Monetary Community
CMA	Common Monetary Area
CARICOM	Caribbean Community and Common Market
DCP	Debt Collection Program
ECB	European Central Bank
ECCB	Eastern Caribbean Central Bank
ECCU	Eastern Caribbean Currency Union
EMS	European Monetary System
EMU	European Economic and Monetary Union
ERM	Exchange rate mechanism
ESCB	European System of Central Banks
EU	European Union
FATF	Financial Action Task Force
FDI	Foreign direct investment
GCC	Cooperation Council for the Arab States of the Gulf
GDP	Gross domestic product
LNG	Liquefied natural gas
OPEC	Organization of Petroleum Exporting Countries
QMR	Qatar monetary rate
REER	Real effective exchange rate
SAMA	Saudi Arabian Monetary Agency
WAMU	West African Monetary Union
WAEC	West African Economic Community
WAEMU	West African Economic and Monetary Union
WTO	World Trade Organization

I Overview

Ugo Fasano

The Heads of States of the Cooperation Council for the Arab States of the Gulf (GCC) decided at the end of 2001 to deepen economic integration by establishing a common currency—pegged to the U.S. dollar—by 2010. This decision represents a practical evolution to the integration efforts that started with the establishment of the GCC in the early 1980s. As an initial step, all GCC countries officially pegged their currencies to the U.S. dollar during 2002 and early 2003 (until then, most currencies of GCC countries had been formally pegged to the SDR). Moreover, a unified regional customs tariff at a single rate of 5 percent became effective in January 2003, while macroeconomic performance criteria will be established by 2005 for the needed policy convergence to support the monetary union. The establishment of an economic and monetary union will create an important regional entity: in 2002 GCC countries had an estimated combined GDP of close to $340 billion, an average weighted per capita nominal GDP of about $12,000, and held some 45 percent and 17 percent, respectively, of the world's proven oil and natural gas reserves (Table 1.1).

In the past two decades, GCC countries have made important progress toward economic and financial integration (See Section II and Appendixes I–III). Formal barriers to the free movement of national goods and workers have been eliminated, individuals and corporations of these countries have been granted national treatment for tax purposes in all GCC countries, and nationals have been recently allowed to invest in stock markets and real estate of most other member states. In addition, GCC countries enjoy low inflation, stable nominal bilateral exchange rates, and similar levels of nominal interest rates, as well as trade and payments systems relatively free of restrictions. They also share a remarkable degree of cultural and political homogeneity.

The move to a monetary union, combined with appropriate macroeconomic and structural policies, is likely to be beneficial for GCC countries. This move should, in particular, improve the efficiency of financial services, lower transaction costs, and increase transparency in prices of goods and services, and thereby facilitate appropriate investment decisions.

In addition, by requiring sustainable fiscal positions, the union should promote a better allocation of resources within the GCC area. Nevertheless, the experience of other monetary unions shows that additional convergence policies are needed to promote stronger ties in other areas and stimulate growth. Section III and Appendix IV review the experiences of these other monetary unions and draw lessons for the GCC countries.

In contrast, the costs of a monetary union—the loss of national monetary and exchange rate policies—should be limited in the foreseeable future, because important shocks are likely to affect GCC countries in a similar way, given the still high importance of oil in their finances and, to a lesser extent, in their economic structure. In addition, these countries share a flexible labor market for expatriate workers (who account for the largest share of the labor force in the non-oil sector). This flexibility has facilitated the adjustment to oil shocks, particularly under a de facto fixed exchange rate regime. Section IV discusses the potential costs and benefits of a monetary union among GCC countries.

Experience, however, suggests that a successful monetary union requires careful political and economic preparation to reduce its potential risks. Above all, a monetary union requires a strong political commitment—as member countries have to give up some sovereignty in the decision-making process—and the ability to adjust domestic economic policies to deal with the effects of a single currency. In fact, giving up national monetary and exchange rate policies could be costly if policy convergence is not sustained. Moreover, possible important changes in economic structure and trade patterns in the long run could mean that individual members of a monetary union may experience different growth and inflation effects after unification. As a result, structural policies that would promote flexibility in labor and product markets assume greater importance in a monetary union. Moreover, member countries of a monetary union need to create a level playing field among themselves to make the union successful over time, including the elimination of nontrade barriers.

Table 1.1. GCC Countries: Selected Economic and Social Indicators, 2002[1]

	Nominal GDP (In millions of U.S. dollars)	Nominal GDP Per Capita (In U.S. dollars)[2]	Population (In millions)[2]	Overall Fiscal Balance (In percent of GDP)[3]	Total Government Gross Debt (In percent of GDP)	Proven Oil Reserves (In years)[4]	Central Bank Foreign Assets (In months of imports)[5]	External Current Account Balance (In percent of GDP)	Life Expectancy at Birth (In years)[6]	Illiteracy (In percent of population, 15+)[6]
Bahrain	8,506	11,619	0.7	0.8	30.3	15	2.9	0.3	73	12
Kuwait	33,215	15,098	2.2	20.6	32.9	134	10.7	20.9	77	18
Oman	20,290	7,515	2.7	3.7	16.0	16	4.8	10.0	74	27
Qatar	17,321	28,362	0.6	8.3	53.4	15	2.8	13.8	75	19
Saudi Arabia	188,960	8,567	22.1	−6.0	97.1	85	9.2	4.7	73	24
United Arab Emirates	71,187	19,613	3.6	−9.3	4.5	124	4.7	5.5	75	24
GCC countries	339,479	11,979[7]	31.9	−2.7[7]	66.6[7]	84[7]	7.7	6.9[7]	75	21

Sources: National authorities; IMF staff estimates; and World Bank (2001).

[1] Based on preliminary information available as of April 2003.
[2] Including expatriates.
[3] Including investment income of government foreign assets.
[4] Based on current production.
[5] These figures are not an accurate reflection of the country's foreign asset position because data on government foreign assets are partial in some GCC countries.
[6] Latest available information.
[7] Weighted average.

GCC countries will therefore still need to make key choices and take important steps to address remaining policy and institutional differences to reap the potential net benefits of a monetary union. Importantly, the adequacy of fiscal policies and initial fiscal stance vary across countries, with the budget structure not very supportive of growth and highly vulnerable to oil price shocks across the GCC area. The incentive policies to promote economic development diverge across countries, creating cases of unfair competition. Restrictions still hinder the development of the government and corporate bond and equity markets in the GCC area. Moreover, the coverage, timeliness, and quality of national statistics, as well as the policy on transparency, differ across countries. Furthermore, the pace of structural reforms also varies across countries, with some already facing rising unemployment.

Fiscal Issues

Maintaining a strong fiscal position and adopting a common code of fiscal conduct—consisting of fiscal convergence criteria, a common accounting framework for public accounts, and adequate budgetary procedures—should receive the highest priority before introducing a common currency. This should be done in order to avoid economic strains and loss of political support, since it would be difficult to sustain a monetary union among countries with significantly divergent macroeconomic conditions and policies. Indeed, in a monetary union, coordinating fiscal policy is necessary to reduce the risk of an undesirable policy mix between member countries' decentralized fiscal policies and the union's centralized monetary stance.

The fiscal convergence criteria should reflect the need to maintain a sustainable fiscal position in all GCC countries, ensuring intergenerational economic equity objectives. However, the choice of fiscal criteria is complex in the case of these countries because of their differences in expenditure rigidity, oil dependency, as well as oil and financial wealth. Section V analyzes the options for implementing a monetary union among the GCC countries.

As a possible fiscal criterion, GCC countries could consider adopting an overall balanced budget target over the medium term based on a similar conservative crude oil price assumption across the membership, with actual surpluses or deficits only reflecting the fluctuations in terms of trade. At the same time, GCC authorities could also establish targets for closely monitoring member countries' non-oil fiscal deficits (including investment income) to determine underlying fiscal trends. A ceiling on government debt, possibly net of certain government liquid assets, could also be an additional fiscal con-

vergence criterion to discourage countries to run ex post overall fiscal deficits for several consecutive years.

Given the volatility in oil prices and, in turn, nominal GDP, GCC countries should carefully review whether the chosen convergence criteria should be measured in percent of GDP, or alternatively, in percent of non-oil GDP, or in a common currency. A broad coverage of government activities that would include the central and local governments, extrabudgetary government funds, and pension funds should also be considered. In addition, sound budgetary practices should be followed in each member country. These practices include transparent recording of all revenues and expenditures in line with internationally accepted standards, as well as framing yearly budgets on a realistic medium-term macroeconomic framework.

Exchange Rate Policy

The GCC authorities have decided to peg the common currency to the U.S. dollar. Nevertheless, other options could be considered in light of possible changing trade patterns over the medium-to-long term—with Europe probably gaining in importance through negotiations under way for a trade arrangement between the two areas—and emerging changes in the economic structure and exports across GCC countries. These options could include pegging to a basket of currencies, or, possibly, adopting a more flexible arrangement. Other decisions about the exchange arrangement must also be made, such as the pooling of each GCC member's foreign reserves, the rate at which to irrevocably fix the bilateral rates, and the adoption of common definition—based on international standards—of foreign reserves.

Data Standards and Transparency

Assessing the success in meeting convergence criteria and adherence to policy objectives would require comparable and transparent macroeconomic and financial statistical information across GCC countries. Therefore, the harmonization of fiscal concepts and data quality based on internationally accepted standards and methods should be given high priority before monetary union takes place. For monetary policy decisions, the common central bank will also have to rely on a set of consistent, harmonized statistics, because these decisions will be based on the economic situation in the GCC area as a whole. Furthermore, such statistics are indispensable for financial market participants, as well as for making appropriate investment decisions.

Institutional Arrangements

A viable monetary union must be accompanied by the creation of a single institution (or supranational monetary authority) with clear responsibility for formulating and conducting a centralized monetary policy. Thus, the creation of a common independent central bank represents the most important institutional change that the GCC countries may face on the road toward a common currency. This change could be implemented on a step-by-step basis during the transition period to the introduction of a common currency. A decentralized approach to organizing central bank responsibilities, like that of the European Economic and Monetary Union (EMU), seems to be the most appropriate in a GCC monetary union given political and practical considerations. Under such an agreement, the common central bank will be responsible for taking monetary policy decisions, overseeing the payment systems, and coordinating efforts toward financial integration. The national GCC central banks will implement these decisions, conduct all or some of the foreign exchange operations, maintain their banking supervisory functions, and issue the common currency, as well as operate national payment systems. The contribution of each GCC member country to the capital and seigniorage distribution of a common central bank will also have to be considered.

A common central bank together with the national central banks will have to apply a common set of monetary policy instruments and put in place the necessary regulatory, legal, and institutional framework. The objective of a monetary union provides a chance to complete the process of shifting to market-based monetary policy instruments in all GCC countries and design them in a way that is conducive to the development of money and securities markets. Thus, establishing common monetary policy instruments and a securities market with some minimum depth and breadth before introducing the monetary union is likely to facilitate orderly and effective conduct of monetary policy when entering the union. A financial crisis management system will also need to be designed to avoid a conflict between any needed liquidity support provided to distressed commercial banks and the regional monetary policy stance.

Structural Reforms

Although the adoption of structural reforms is desirable independently of the introduction of a monetary union, they are likely to enhance the positive effects of the common currency. Thus, GCC authorities should give priority to strengthening national labor policies by reducing domestic market segmentation between expatriate and local workers in terms of sectors of employment, wages, and skills, while facilitating cross-border labor mobility of GCC nationals. In addition, priority should be given to reforms that strengthen product market competition, such as anti-trust, commercial, and agency laws, and business codes and regulations. A reform of the welfare and incentive systems would also be desirable to reduce waste and improve the allocation of resources. Moreover, progress should be made in harmonizing or coordinating taxes and pension systems, as well as addressing rigidities in government expenditures.

The GCC countries should also take steps to facilitate the development of the bond and equity markets in the proposed monetary union. These include the harmonizing or coordination of national capital taxation, legislation (e.g., limits on foreign ownership of stocks), and accounting rules related to the holding and trading of securities and equities, as well as in putting in place integrated securities settlement systems. GCC countries should also facilitate the trend toward cross-border banking consolidation that will likely take place in a monetary union, while also focusing on enhancing corporate governance and transparency.

II Progress Toward Economic Integration and Convergence Among GCC Countries

Ugo Fasano

Over the past two decades, the GCC countries have taken important steps to achieve economic and financial integration among them. They have lifted formal impediments to the free movement of national goods, labor, and capital across these countries, and have similar policy preferences in a number of areas. In particular, these countries have been successful in maintaining price and nominal exchange rate stability, as well as an open trade regime and liberal capital flows. In addition, they have in place an open-border foreign labor policy to ensure sufficient supply of labor at internationally competitive wages, with expatriate workers accounting for the largest share of the labor force in non-oil activities. The GCC countries' success in maintaining for several decades a de facto fixed exchange rate in the face of significant global crude oil volatility owes much to this policy framework.[1] Furthermore, since the early 1990s, these countries have devoted increased attention to structural and institutional reforms to encourage diversification, enhance non-oil growth, and develop human capital.[2] However, some differences in economic performance and policy preference have emerged over the past decade (Figure 2.1). Some GCC countries have also been more successful than others in promoting non-oil activities and diversifying exports and government revenue (Figures 2.2 and 2.3).

Inflation

Inflation, as measured by the consumer price index (CPI), has traditionally been low in the GCC area, but it differs across countries.[3] From 1991 to 2002, Bahrain, Oman, and Saudi Arabia experienced the lowest consumer price inflation in the region—less than 1 percent a year on average. In the same period, the United Arab Emirates experienced the highest consumer price inflation—3.5 percent a year. As a result, inflation differentials have led to diverging paths for CPI-based real effective exchange rates (REER) during the past decade, with Kuwait, Qatar, and the United Arab Emirates experiencing appreciation, Oman, depreciation, and the other GCC countries, relatively stable REERs (Figure 2.4).[4]

Real GDP Performance

Disparities in real aggregate GDP growth have also been observed across GCC countries. The economies of Bahrain, Qatar, and the United Arab Emirates have been growing solidly, particularly during the second half of the 1990s, with growth in Oman accelerating over 2000–02. By contrast, growth in Saudi Arabia has been sluggish, while in Kuwait it has practically stagnated since 1997. Much of this difference has reflected the pace of diversification, as well as changes in oil output growth—oil export volumes of most GCC countries, except Bahrain and Oman, are subject to OPEC quota constraints. Meanwhile, except in Qatar, per capita GDP has not grown significantly in the past few years owing in part to continued rapid population growth (Figure 2.5).

---

[1]It is estimated that foreign workers currently account for more than 60 percent of the labor force in the GCC area.

[2]See Appendix I for a description of economic developments in each GCC country from 1990 to 2002.

[3]Movements in the real effective exchange rates should be interpreted with care because of concerns about the quality of consumer price data in some GCC countries.

[4]Most currencies of GCC countries have been formally pegged to the SDR, except the rial Omani, which has been pegged to the U.S. dollar since the 1970s, and the Kuwaiti dinar, which has been pegged to an undisclosed basket of currencies of its main trade and financial partners. However, de facto, most GCC currencies have been pegged to the U.S. dollar at a fixed parity for much of the past two decades. Since 2002 and early 2003, all these currencies have become officially pegged to the U.S. dollar in line with GCC countries' commitments in the road toward a monetary union.

Figure 2.1. GCC Countries: Selected Economic Indicators
(Average 1998–2002 unless otherwise indicated)

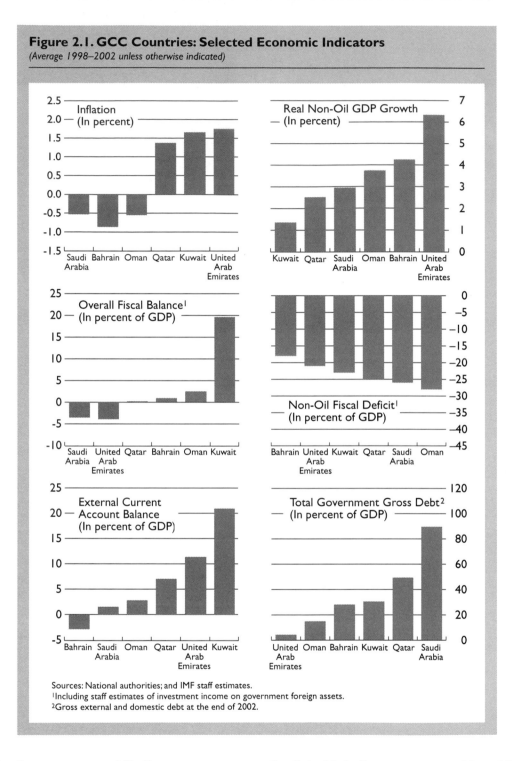

Sources: National authorities; and IMF staff estimates.
[1]Including staff estimates of investment income on government foreign assets.
[2]Gross external and domestic debt at the end of 2002.

Fiscal Performance and Policy

Fiscal performance has varied among the GCC countries in the 1990s. In the first half of the decade, all GCC countries recorded large fiscal deficits as a result of a declining trend in global oil prices and relatively high expenditure. In the process, Qatar and

Saudi Arabia built up government debt, while in other GCC countries government debt remained low as a percent of GDP because the authorities drew down official foreign assets to finance fiscal imbalances. Since the mid-1990s, Kuwait and Oman, and more recently Qatar, have usually registered, on average, an overall fiscal surplus (including investment income),

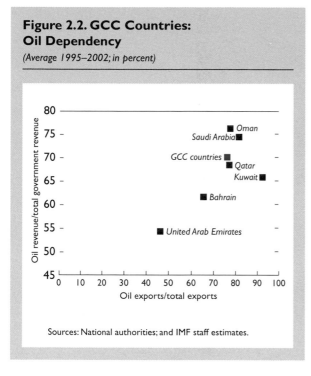

Figure 2.2. GCC Countries: Oil Dependency
(Average 1995–2002; in percent)

Sources: National authorities; and IMF staff estimates.

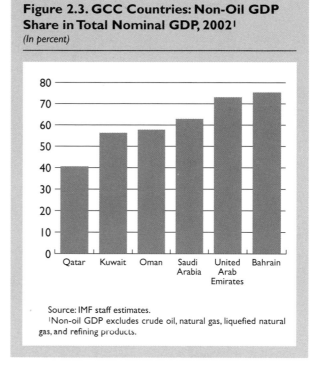

Figure 2.3. GCC Countries: Non-Oil GDP Share in Total Nominal GDP, 2002[1]
(In percent)

Source: IMF staff estimates.
[1]Non-oil GDP excludes crude oil, natural gas, liquefied natural gas, and refining products.

owing mainly to restrained spending. Strong oil prices during 1999–2000 contributed to a temporary sharp improvement in all GCC countries' fiscal positions, despite rising spending.[5] Following weaker global oil prices in 2001–02, the overall fiscal balance switched to a deficit in the largest GCC countries, and the surplus narrowed significantly in the others.

Steps taken over the past several years to reduce the vulnerability of government budget to variations in oil prices through increases in non-oil revenue and restrained spending growth have met with mixed results. Indeed, the non-oil fiscal balance—a useful indicator of underlying fiscal trends in oil-exporting countries because it abstracts from fluctuations in crude oil prices—has worsened significantly in the past few years in some GCC countries, mainly reflecting higher spending (see Figure 2.1).[6]

Over the past decade or so, most GCC countries have pursued a procyclical expenditure policy, which has led to a rigid expenditure structure.[7] The scope and budgetary impact of the subsidies and a generous welfare system have remained relatively high. Moreover, social welfare policies manifested in generous benefit packages to nationals have led to large wage bills as a percent of GDP by international standards (Figure 2.6). In addition, defense spending measured in per capita terms or in percent of GDP is also among the highest in the world. Furthermore, despite the high dependence on volatile oil revenue, few GCC countries have adopted a budgetary policy in a medium-term framework to delink public expenditure decisions from the evolution of short-term oil revenue. Also, the development of non-oil activities has not generated a corresponding increase in non-oil revenue partly because of the use of tax exemptions and holidays, and delays in adopting a modern tax system by all GCC countries (Figure 2.7). Important differences remain regarding the tax treatment of non-GCC individuals and corporations across the area (Appendix II). Nevertheless, the recent trend in the area is toward equal tax treatment of foreign and local companies to attract foreign investment.

External Sector Performance

External current account developments also indicate considerable differences among GCC countries. Kuwait and the United Arab Emirates recorded sizable current account surpluses during much of the 1990s, even in 1998 when average crude oil prices

---

[5]The comparison of fiscal developments across GCC countries is hindered by the (partial) exclusion in some of them of certain revenues and expenditures from the central government's budget.

[6]The non-oil or nonhydrocarbon fiscal balance is defined as non-oil (and gas) revenue, including investment income on government assets, minus total expenditure, including net lending.

[7]See Fasano and Wang (2002) for an analysis of the relationship between government revenue and expenditure in GCC countries.

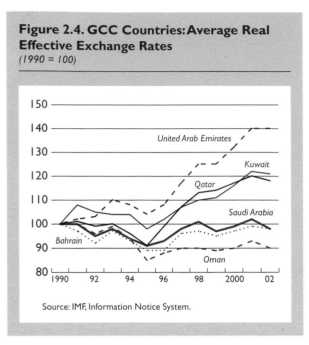

Figure 2.4. GCC Countries: Average Real Effective Exchange Rates
(1990 = 100)

Source: IMF, Information Notice System.

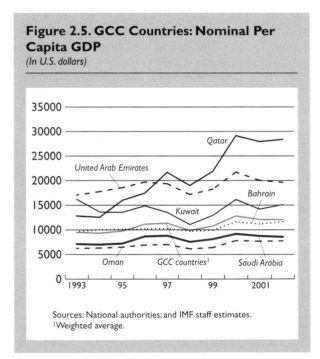

Figure 2.5. GCC Countries: Nominal Per Capita GDP
(In U.S. dollars)

Sources: National authorities; and IMF staff estimates.
[1]Weighted average.

collapsed to less than $12 a barrel. The strong recovery in oil prices in 1999–2000 contributed to strengthening other GCC countries' external positions. This recovery was compounded in Qatar and Oman by rapidly rising exports of liquefied natural gas (LNG) beginning in late 1996 and 2000, respectively. However, some GCC countries are estimated to have

shifted back to external current account deficits in 2002, as a result of weaker global oil prices and cuts in oil output. The foreign assets of GCC central banks have usually remained at over three months of imports of goods and services, even in periods of low oil prices, as fiscal and externals imbalances have been usually reflected in changes in government foreign assets. External debt in percent of GDP is quite low in the GCC area, except in Qatar, which borrowed heavily in the 1990s to finance LNG and industrial projects (Figure 2.8).[8] In addition, the level of intra-GCC trade remains modest (between 1997 and 2001, about one-third of non-oil GCC exports (including reexports) was traded among GCC countries).

Monetary Performance and Policy

The lack of monetary autonomy—under liberal capital flows and the pegged exchange rate regime in place in GCC countries—has resulted in similar nominal short-term interest rates across the area and in a narrow spread over comparable U.S. securities, except in Kuwait (Figure 2.9).[9] In the latter, probably reflecting a higher exchange rate risk under a basket peg, interbank interest rates have been, on average, 100 basis points above similar U.S. dollar–denominated assets during the second half of the 1990s—compared with less than 20 basis points on average for other GCC countries over the same period—though it has narrowed significantly in the past few years. However, because of inflation differentials, real interest rates have varied across GCC countries.

Although these countries have gradually taken a number of steps to enhance their capacity to implement a market-based monetary policy, differences remain in the set of monetary instruments currently in place across the GCC area. Bahrain, in particular, has made a relatively rapid and smooth transition to using indirect instruments for liquidity management through the sale of government paper and secondary market operations consisting mainly of repos with commercial banks. Oman and the United Arab Emirates partially rely on issuance of certificates of deposits by the central bank to control liquidity. Other GCC countries implement monetary policy by applying reserve requirements and through the use of prudential ratios (such as loans/deposits ratio) to penalize excessive lending. Direct instruments (interest

---

[8]The Qatar government has guaranteed about one-third of the LNG debt, while the LNG debt servicing is tied to its export proceeds.

[9]Because of the lack of autonomy, most central banks in the GCC area manage overall liquidity in the banking system in a relatively passive manner.

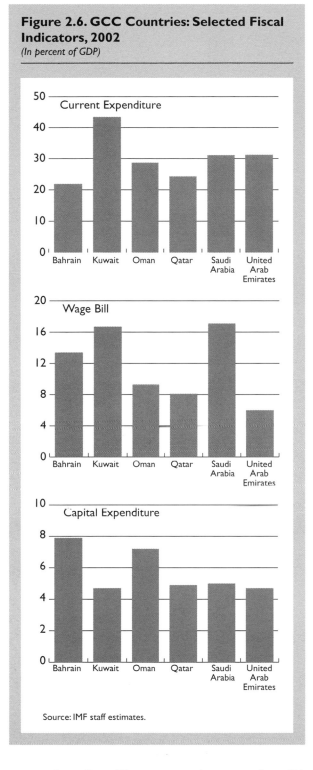

Figure 2.6. GCC Countries: Selected Fiscal Indicators, 2002
(In percent of GDP)

Source: IMF staff estimates.

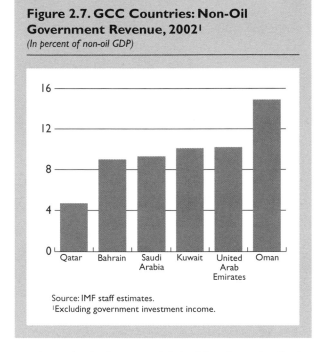

Figure 2.7. GCC Countries: Non-Oil Government Revenue, 2002[1]
(In percent of non-oil GDP)

Source: IMF staff estimates.
[1]Excluding government investment income.

pendence is de facto established by the strict limits or even prohibition in a few cases on central bank lending to the government (Table 2.1). In addition, the price and exchange rate stability objectives, liberal capital flows, as well as large foreign financial assets in some countries have insulated the national central banks from pressures created by the governments' need to finance fiscal deficits.

The Financial Sector

The GCC countries share sound and well-supervised banking systems. Indeed, across the area, banks are well capitalized and profitable, and comply with prudential regulations. Moreover, the improved trend in the asset quality of the banks' portfolio has been a key development in some GCC countries, particularly since the mid-1990s. In addition, the number of Islamic banks is increasing in the GCC area. The supervisory framework in all these countries has been strengthened and continues to be strengthened, while they seem to be largely compliant with most principles of international standards and codes, including anti-money laundering and the combating of terrorism financing.[10] However, differences remain in bank

rate and credit ceilings on certain types of credit) continue to play some role in Kuwait and Oman.

Central bank independence is not yet officially enshrined in the law of any GCC country. Nevertheless, in most of these countries, considerable inde-

---

[10]In 2001 the United Arab Emirates completed a joint World Bank–IMF Financial Sector Assessment Program (FSAP). The Financial System Stability Assessment report is available on the IMF's public website (http://www.imf.org/external/pubs/cat). In the first half of 2003, an FSAP was under way in Oman.

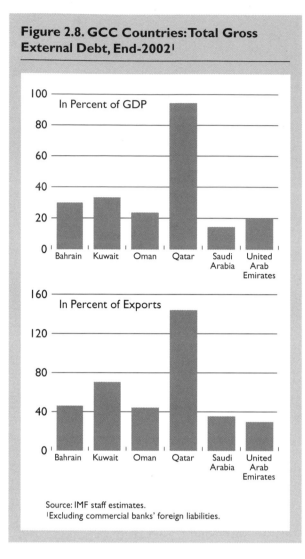

Figure 2.8. GCC Countries: Total Gross External Debt, End-2002[1]

In Percent of GDP

In Percent of Exports

Source: IMF staff estimates.
[1]Excluding commercial banks' foreign liabilities.

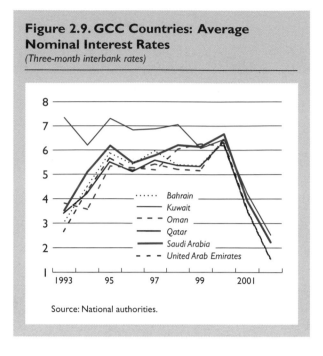

Figure 2.9. GCC Countries: Average Nominal Interest Rates
(Three-month interbank rates)

Bahrain
Kuwait
Oman
Qatar
Saudi Arabia
United Arab Emirates

Source: National authorities.

regulatory practices, particularly regarding entry restrictions, liquidity requirements, loan classification and provisioning, and ownership, preventing full integration of the region's financial and capital markets. In addition, with the exception of Saudi Arabia, the region's equity markets are still relatively small and underdeveloped, while private securities markets are nascent in all GCC countries. Most GCC countries, except Oman, limit foreign investment in equity through mutual funds.

Structural Reforms and the Labor Market

GCC countries are currently at various stages of implementing structural and institutional reforms—including financial deepening—that aim at

establishing the foundations for private sector–led and outward oriented growth (Appendix III). Although full privatization of existing government companies has not been embraced in most GCC countries, a number of steps have been taken to promote private investment. In particular, substantial progress has been made in the regulatory, institutional, and legal frameworks governing foreign direct investment in all GCC countries. In fact, 100 percent foreign ownership of companies is allowed in most (non-oil) sectors, including utilities. To spur intra-GCC trade, local products that are made by fully foreign-owned companies now enjoy the same benefits as those owned by GCC nationals.[11]

While GCC economies are generally characterized by labor market segmentation—between nationals and expatriates in terms of sector of employment, wages, nonwage benefits, and skills—the labor market challenges differ across countries. A rapidly growing number of young nationals are currently entering the labor force, particularly in Bahrain, Oman, and Saudi Arabia. With nationals protected, in practice, by relatively more restrictive dismissal regulations and a downward rigidity of wages, a flexible labor market for expatriates has remained an essential policy instrument to adjust to

---

[11]Until late 1999, firms had to be majority national owned for their products to be exempt from tariffs when crossing the border from one GCC member state to another.

Table 2.1. Overview of Key Elements of GCC Central Bank Laws

	Bahrain	Kuwait	Oman	Qatar	Saudi Arabia	United Arab Emirates
Objectives	Maintain the value of the currency, ensure monetary stability, and control and direct credit so as to realize the economic policy objectives of the state.	Secure currency stability and direct credit policy so as to assist social and economic progress and growth of national income.	Maintain the domestic and international value of the currency and promote the development of banking institutions to ensure the maintenance of financial stability and contribute to the economic, industrial, and financial growth of the Sultanate.	Safeguard the internal and external value of the currency and promote exchange conditions conducive to the growth of the national economy within the framework of monetary stability.	Stabilize the internal and external value of the currency and take measures to strengthen the currency's cover.	Maintain stability of the currency internally and externally and achieve a steady growth of the national economy.
Central bank financing of government deficits	Only temporary advances not to exceed 10 percent of the budget revenues for the preceding year. To be repaid no later than three months after the end of the fiscal year.	Only temporary advances not to exceed 10 percent of public revenue for the preceding fiscal year. No further advances if loans are not repaid by the end of the fiscal year.	Only temporary advances not to exceed 10 percent (including face value of outstanding treasury bills) of the estimated recurrent revenues. To be repaid within 90 days.	Not explicitly mentioned in the Act.	Prohibited.	Interest-free advances to the government allowed in any year, but not to exceed 10 percent of government revenues in the previous year. To be repaid no later than at the end of the financial year.
Rules for cover through foreign reserves	100 percent of the currency in circulation. In exceptional circumstances this can be lowered to 75 percent.	100 percent of monetary base.	Cover of monetary base is to be prescribed by the Board of Governors, subject to approval by His Majesty the Sultan.	100 percent cover of currency in circulation (can be lowered for up to six months).	100 percent cover of currency in circulation (Currency Law).	70 percent of monetary base.
Terms of office of decision-making authority	Five years for Board, consisting of the Prime Minister as the Chairman, the Minister of Finance, a representative of the Ministry of Finance, and three other members.	Five years for Governor and Deputy Governor; three years for four other members; no fixed terms for two Ministry of Finance representatives.	Overlapping, renewable five-year terms for all seven members of the Board of Governors.	Five years for Governor and Deputy Governor; three years for the other three members.	Five years for all five members of the Board of Directors.	Four years for all members of the Board of Directors that may be renewed several times.
Procedures for appointment	The representative of the Ministry of Finance and the three other members are appointed by Amiri Decree on the recommendation of the Minister of Finance.	Governor, Deputy Governor, and four other members are appointed by the Council of Ministers on the recommendation of the Minister of Finance.	Members of the Board of Governors are appointed by His Majesty the Sultan.	Appointed by decree on the recommendation of the Minister of Finance.	Governor and three Board members appointed by royal decree. Vice Governor appointed by royal decree on the nomination of the Minister of Finance and approval of the Council of Ministers.	Appointed by a union decree after approval of the Council of Ministers.
General criteria for removal defined	Yes.	Yes.	Yes.	Yes.	No.	Yes.
Date of central bank law	1973	1968	2000	1973 (new draft law under review).	1957	1980 (new draft law under review).

Source: Based on central bank laws of GCC countries.

oil price shocks in GCC countries in the context of a de facto fixed exchange regime. On institutional issues, important differences across countries exist regarding commercial agencies, industrial licensing, bankruptcy laws and regulations, and government tenders and contracts. Similar formal protection for patent, copyright, and trademark name protection and intellectual property rights is, however, becoming the rule following most GCC countries' membership in the World Trade Organization (WTO). On real estate ownership, rules permitting GCC nationals to own property in any GCC country have been significantly relaxed in the past few years.[12]

Data Issues

Progress has been uneven across GCC countries in improving the quality, timeliness, and dissemination of economic and financial data, and in adopting international standards.[13] Thus, despite strong economic fundamentals, the external borrowing cost of governments in the GCC area has been high.[14] This has been reflected, for instance, in relatively large sovereign bond spreads (350 basis points or higher) at times in the case of Qatar because of "information risk," as perceived by international capital markets (see Figure A1.5 in Appendix I).

---

[12]In the United Arab Emirates, the Emirate of Dubai has been at the forefront of allowing foreign ownership of real estate through long-term leases.

---

[13]As of June 2003, only Kuwait and Oman participate in the IMF's General Data Dissemination System.

[14]Only the governments of Oman and Qatar have accessed through end-2002 international capital markets mostly to finance infrastructure and other projects.

III Main Lessons from the Experience of Monetary Unions

Rina Bhattacharya and Ugo Fasano

In a "full" monetary union, independent nation states adopt a single monetary policy and a common currency. This is characterized by a single external exchange rate policy, as well as the permanent absence of all exchange controls, whether for current or capital transactions. By contrast, a "pseudo"-monetary union—in some aspects currently the case among GCC countries—is an agreement to maintain fixed exchange rates among the member states, but without explicit integration of economic policy, a common pool of foreign exchange reserves, and a single monetary policy. Moreover, the institutional framework and the tools to maintain exchange rates permanently fixed do not exist in a pseudo-monetary union. Thus, there is always the possibility that one or more member countries could have a strong incentive to allow its exchange rate to depreciate or appreciate against the others if under pressure. The expectation that this may happen will likely prevent complete monetary integration.

There are five monetary unions in the world at present (Table 3.1). Three of these unions are in Africa, one in the Caribbean, and one in Europe (the euro area—see Appendix IV for further details.) In all of them, a new common currency was created, except in the Southern African Common Monetary Area (CMA), in which the rand, the South African currency, is the common currency in circulation.[1] It is interesting to note that while the euro area countries adopted a common market before a currency union, the others reversed the order: they are now in the process of moving toward full economic integration, after having a monetary union in place for several decades.

The following policy lessons from the experience of these unions can be relevant for the GCC countries.[2]

- The main challenges involved in achieving monetary integration is the adoption of both economic and political measures to promote greater intraregional economic integration, with currency unification being only one of several components of a much broader regional integration efforts. Clearly, greater economic integration has to go hand in hand with greater political integration.

- A political consensus will need to be reached on several issues. These include the institutional framework and policy guidelines for a common independent central bank, the sharing of seigniorage revenue from a common currency, and the institutional and policy framework to promote macroeconomic stability in each of the member nations, including the adoption of an institutional mechanism for fiscal transfers to cushion the impact of asymmetric shocks on the member states of the monetary union.

- A viable monetary union should be accompanied by the creation of a single institution or (supranational monetary authority) with clear responsibility for formulating and conducting monetary policy. In all the monetary unions, a common central bank has been given monopoly power over monetary policy.

- Some monetary unions have been initially organized around a strong, credible, and already existing central bank within the union. For instance, prior to the establishment of the European Central Bank (ECB), the Deutsche Bundesbank provided the initial monetary stability for what later became the euro area in the context of a flexible exchange rate regime choice for the common currency. This was also the case in monetary unions with asymmetry in the size of their member countries, with the largest country usually having effective control over the common monetary policy, as, for example, South Africa in the CMA. More symmetric monetary unions with relatively weaker institutions have created a common central bank and

---

[1]The CMA is considered an example of an "asymmetric" monetary union, whereby one member country takes a leadership role. There are also "implicit" or "unilateral" monetary unions among countries that have chosen to adopt as a medium of exchange the currency of another country, such as the U.S. dollar.

[2]Based on Masson and Pattillo (2001).

Table 3.1. Main Characteristics of Monetary Unions

	ECCU[1]	WAEMU[2]	CAEMC[3]	Euro Area[4]	CMA[5]	GCC[6]
Number of countries	8	8	6	12	4	6
Single currency?	Yes (Eastern Caribbean dollar).	Yes (CFA franc).	Yes (CFA franc).	Yes (euro).	No (but South African rand circulates in all).	Yes.
Common central bank?	Yes (ECCB).	Yes (BCEAO).	Yes (BEAC).	Yes (ECB), but national central banks execute monetary policy.	No (but South African Reserve Bank has considerable influence).	Not yet decided.
Common pool of reserves?	Yes.	Yes.	Yes.	Yes.	No.	Not yet decided.
Free trade area?	No.	No.	No.	Yes.	Yes.	Yes.[7]
Common external tariff?	No.	Yes.	Yes, in principle.	Yes.	Yes.	Yes.[7]
External current account convertibility?	Yes.	Yes (assured by French Treasury).	Yes (assured by French Treasury).	Yes.	Yes.	Yes.
Degree of capital mobility within region	Moderate.	Low, though in principle free.	Low, though in principle free.	High.	High.	In principle free.
External exchange rate anchor?	Yes (peg to U.S. dollar).	Yes (peg to euro).	Yes (peg to euro).	No.	No.	Yes (peg to U.S. dollar).
Ratio of per capita GDP of richest to poorest country in the area	3.2	4.7	20.0	4.0	8.1	5.2

Source: Reproduced and updated from Table 5.1 in Masson and Pattillo (2001).

[1]The Eastern Caribbean Currency Union (ECCU) includes Anguilla, Antigua and Barbuda, Dominica, Grenada, Montserrat, St. Kitts and Nevis, St. Lucia, and St. Vincent and the Grenadines.
[2]The West African Economic and Monetary Union (WAEMU) includes Benin, Burkina Faso, Côte d'Ivoire, Guinea-Bissau, Mali, Niger, Senegal, and Togo.
[3]The Central African Economic and Monetary Community (CAEMC) includes Cameroon, Chad, the Central African Republic, the Republic of Congo, Equatorial Guinea, and Gabon.
[4]The euro area includes Austria, Belgium, Finland, France, Germany, Greece, Ireland, Italy, Luxembourg, the Netherlands, Portugal, and Spain.
[5]The Common Monetary Area (CMA) includes Lesotho, Namibia, South Africa, and Swaziland. The CMA could be considered a quasi-monetary union.
[6]Expected to be established by 2010.
[7]Single common external tariff was established in January 2003.

relied on an external nominal anchor. In the Eastern Caribbean Currency Union (ECCU), the common currency was initially pegged to the pound sterling and later to the U.S. dollar, and in two of the unions in Africa, initially to the French franc and currently to the euro.

- A viable and effective union needs reinforced surveillance over the fiscal policies of its members to ensure the compatibility of individual member countries' fiscal stance with the overall objectives of monetary policy set for the zone as a whole. In addition, adopting clear sanctions on the fiscal policy side could be very important to encourage fiscal discipline. There is also a strong case for establishing an institutional framework to minimize the chances of any member country (or group of countries) of a monetary union adopting unsustainable fiscal policies.

- A successful monetary union will need to prevent systemic crises in the financial sector through the development of a strong regulatory and supervisory framework for the domestic and regional financial markets.

- A monetary union on its own cannot enhance growth prospects without favorable supporting structural reforms that aim at strengthening domestic institutions, including governance and transparency.

Considerable differences in terms of institutional and legal structures, however, exist among the current monetary unions. In Europe, integration has given rise to intergovernmental bodies, with clear supranational authority in particular areas, while in some other unions supranationality has been limited to the common central bank. In addition, the unions also differ greatly in terms of the degree of capital mobility, export growth, GDP per capita, inflation, as well as fiscal and external performance.[3] In fact, even long-standing monetary unions have not been able to completely achieve fiscal convergence.[4] Nevertheless, recent experiences with monetary unions provide empirical support for the importance of establishing a credible institutional and policy framework for enhancing macroeconomic stability in each of the member countries, and the need for greater economic integration to go hand in hand with greater political integration.

---

[3]Price stability is however a feature of the way the monetary policy is anchored, and whether there are adequate safeguards against excessive monetary expansion, rather than the result of a monetary union per se.

[4]Fiscal divergence was probably possible because, for instance, some monetary unions in Africa have had the strong financial backing of France. See Doré and Masson (2002) for an analysis of achieving fiscal convergence in monetary unions in Africa.

IV   Potential Benefits and Costs of a Common Currency for GCC Countries

Andrea Schaechter

Why do countries decide to join or form a monetary union? The literature on optimum currency areas, initiated by Mundell's seminal paper (1961), has extensively discussed the potential benefits and costs of monetary unions.[1] Countries can gain from a monetary union through lower transaction costs and the elimination of exchange rate variability, spurring investment, intraregional trade, and economic growth. Other benefits are access to bigger financial markets—lowering borrowing costs—and the potential enforcement of monetary and fiscal discipline. The main costs are the loss of national monetary and exchange rate policies. The magnitude of those costs depends on how symmetrical the economies are in terms of business cycles and vulnerability to shocks and the ease with which the economies can adjust to disturbances. These costs are likely to be lower the higher the degree of labor market flexibility across the member countries. In addition, political objectives can also be the driving force behind joining or forming a monetary union. Establishing a regional economic and political power bloc can result in a bigger role in world financial markets for the region as a whole. Other political incentives may include delegating to an institution outside the domestic political process the enforcement of monetary and fiscal discipline (Mundell, 1997).

For the GCC countries, moving to a full monetary union—by fixing bilateral exchange rates irrevocably and introducing a common currency—from the current pseudo-monetary-union arrangement—stable nominal bilateral exchange rates—is likely to be beneficial in several aspects. Although direct gains, such as increased intraregional trade from the union, might be relatively small for these countries, indirect gains should be more significant. The planned monetary union should reinforce the beneficial effects of the ongoing and planned structural and institutional reforms to better face the challenges of diversifying the economy and generating employment opportunities for a rapidly rising domestic labor force. The monetary union may also enhance a mutual surveillance mechanism, enforcing in particular fiscal discipline across the membership. In addition, it will likely increase price transparency, facilitating appropriate investment decisions across the GCC area. However, the most important benefit of introducing a common currency among GCC countries will most likely be the integration and development of the area's bond, equity, and money markets, improving the efficiency of financial services, and in turn (non-oil) growth prospects (see "Potential Benefits from a Monetary Union" below).

In contrast, the main costs of a monetary union—giving up the ability to set independent national monetary and exchange rate policies—should be limited because important exogenous shocks (such as crude oil price changes) would affect GCC countries in a similar way given the still high importance of oil in their economies. Indeed, fluctuations in crude oil price changes have induced comparable effects on the GCC countries' external current account and fiscal positions (Table 4.1). Moreover, high labor market flexibility in GCC countries has also contributed to the relative ease of adjusting to oil shocks under a fixed exchange rate regime—though this flexibility applies only to the large segment of expatriate workers employed in non-oil activities in these countries. In addition, GCC countries have not relied on monetary and exchange rate tools for quite some time under their pegged exchange rate regimes. Overall, the GCC countries seem well positioned to successfully form and sustain a full monetary union. But the union will need to be supported by appropriate macroeconomic policies, a range of structural reforms, and strong political commitment to be fully effective and beneficial for its members. Moreover, the institutional framework will have to be carefully designed to keep the costs of a monetary union low.

[1]For a survey of the optimum currency area literature see, for example, Masson and Taylor (1993). Attempts to estimate the benefits and costs for monetary unions have been made by, among others, De Grauwe and Vanhaverbeke (1991), Bayoumi and Eichengreen (1994), Mélitz and Weber (1996), Rose (2000), and Persson (2001).

Table 4.1. GCC Countries: Actual Impact of Recent Oil Price Changes on Selected Indicators
(In percentage points of GDP, unless otherwise indicated)

	Bahrain	Kuwait	Oman	Qatar	Saudi Arabia	United Arab Emirates
Oil price decline, 1998; change in:[1]						
Crude oil exports	−3.0	−11.4	−10.3	7.1	−10.0	−7.9
Total imports (in percent)	−13.2	−0.4	12.2	−3.1	4.2	−4.7
Current account balance						
(− = deterioration)[2]	−12.0	−17.8	−20.6	4.9	−9.2	−8.7
Non-oil real GDP growth[3,4]	0.7	−1.0	−3.9	−12.3	−2.7	−4.2
Overall fiscal balance						
(− = deterioration)	−0.6	−17.8	−9.9	−1.4	−6.4	−9.2
Fiscal policy[5]						
Government expenditure	0.8	1.7	3.2	−0.8	−1.0	6.2
Current	0.9	1.9	2.5	−0.5	1.0	3.7
Development[6]	−0.1	−0.3	0.7	−0.2	−2.0	2.5
Non-oil revenue[7]	1.2	0.4	2.0	0.2	3.8	1.4
Total government gross debt	5.6	5.9	7.3	7.3	25.0	2.2
Oil price increase, 2000; change in:[8]						
Crude oil exports	4.3	12.9	9.7	4.4	9.7	6.1
Total imports (in percent)	25.7	−3.8	6.9	7.6	7.8	9.4
Current account balance						
(+ = improvement)	6.5	23.7	15.7	15.5	7.3	15.0
Non-oil real GDP growth[3]	1.2	0.1	2.7	1.6	0.8	2.2
Overall fiscal balance						
(+ = improvement)	15.5	10.0	8.8	10.4	9.2	11.6
Fiscal policy[5]						
Government expenditure	−2.7	−0.1	−3.1	−5.6	2.8	−4.7
Current	−1.7	0.2	−2.5	−11.7	1.8	−1.1
Development[6]	−1.0	−0.3	−0.6	−0.9	1.0	−3.4
Non-oil revenue[7]	−1.4	1.7	−2.2	1.7	−0.9	−1.2
Total government gross debt	−0.1	−12.7	−6.7	−12.0	−16.3	−2.7

Source: IMF staff estimates based on data from national authorities.
[1]Change vis-à-vis 1997.
[2]The improvement in Qatar reflects higher export volume of liquefied natural gas and crude oil.
[3]Percentage points; excluding oil, natural gas, and refineries.
[4]The sharp deceleration in growth in Qatar reflects the completion of several projects.
[5]Negative sign = decline; positive sign = increase.
[6]Including net lending.
[7]Excluding government investment income.
[8]Change vis-à-vis 1999.

Potential Benefits from a Monetary Union

A monetary union among GCC countries can serve as a catalyst for stronger integration and deepening of financial markets if the introduction of a common currency is accompanied by the full liberalization of financial markets across its members.[2]

Integration of Money Markets

A single currency can foster the integration of interbank money markets across GCC countries, but at the same time, it is also a precondition for effectively

---

[2]While there have been numerous theoretical and empirical studies on the effects of monetary unions on the real economy, the impact on financial integration has hardly been discussed other than under the scenario of a common market. The European Central Bank (ECB), however, has conducted a detailed assessment of the impact of the euro on money, bonds, and equity markets. See ECB (2001a, 2001b, and 2001c); and Santillán, Bayle, and Thygesen (2000).

Table 4.2. GCC Countries: Monetary Policy Instruments

	Bahrain	Kuwait	Oman	Qatar	Saudi Arabia	United Arab Emirates
Direct instruments						
Interest rate controls	None.	Yes. Ceilings on all lending rates tied to discount rate. For loans of up to one year the rate is 250 basis points above the discount rate; and for loans exceeding one year, 400 basis points above.	Yes. Interest rate ceiling on personal loans (11 percent).	None. Long-term rates for small projects are subsidized.	None. Long-term rates are subsidized.	None. Mortgage rates are subsidized.
Directed loans	Development/specialized banks direct credit to specific sectors.	None.	Development bank directs credit to specific sectors. Long-term rates are subsidized.	Development bank directs credit to specific sectors.	Public credit institutions direct credit to specific sectors.	Government credit to specific sectors.
Credit ceilings and others[1]	None.	None.	Maximum of personal loans set at 40 percent of total bank lending. Maximum of 5 percent of bank's net worth for any nonresident individual borrower in foreign currency. Maximum of 30 percent of bank's net worth for all loans to nonresidents in foreign currency.	Bank credit to any one country should not exceed 20 percent of the bank's capital and reserves. Banks are not allowed to lend more than 20 percent of the total value of a real estate project.	None.	None.
Indirect instruments						
Reserve requirements	Yes, unremunerated; 5 percent on dinar deposits.	Yes, unremunerated; reserve ratio based on maturity.	Yes, unremunerated; 5 percent on domestic and foreign currency deposits.	Yes, unremunerated; cash reserves of 2.75 percent of total deposits (including foreign deposits).	Yes, unremunerated; 7 percent on demand deposits and 2 percent on time deposits.	Yes, unremunerated; 1 percent on time deposits and 14 percent on current deposits.
Open market operations	Repos with treasury bills; foreign exchange swaps.	Liquidity scheme; foreign exchange swaps; deposit operations.	Repos. Foreign exchange swaps.	Periodic repo operations and deposit facility (Qatar monetary rate mechanism).	Repos are most important instrument. Foreign exchange swaps.	Foreign exchange swaps. Repos/reverse repos to be developed.
Central bank paper	No.	No.	Yes.	No.	No.	Yes.
Memorandum item:						
Primary market sales of government securities through central bank	Yes, treasury bills and development bonds.	Yes, treasury bills and government bonds.	Yes, treasury bills and developments bonds.	Yes, treasury bills and government bonds.	Yes, treasury bills and government bonds.	No, federal and local governments have not issued securities.

Source: IMF staff based on information from national authorities.

[1]Tradional credit ceilings have been eliminated. The remaining ceilings have regulatory purposes with the aim of financial sector stability.

conducting a common monetary policy. Since monetary policy is set at a regional level, and the liquidity is managed for the region as a whole, money markets need to redistribute the liquidity within the region in a way that leads to a common short-term yield curve. Cross-border arbitrage ensures that monetary stimuli are felt by the entire banking system. Establishing an efficient, fully integrated payment system is key to facilitating cross-border payments and the integration of money markets. The necessary harmonization of monetary policy instruments, and complete move to market-based instruments, can also contribute to money market development. At present, monetary policy instruments in GCC countries are not all market-based and often not designed in a way that is conducive to the development of money and securities markets (Table 4.2). For example, Oman applies ceilings on personal loans lending rates (set at 11 percent in early 2003), and Kuwait on all types of loans—though rates are frequently revised. The United Arab Emirates operates mostly through the issuance of central bank certificates of deposit at the initiative of banks. Since these certificates can be sold back to the central bank any time at a very low penalty, interbank activities have been discouraged.

Integration of Bond and Equity Markets

A monetary union for the GCC countries could also contribute to the integration and development of the region's bond and equity markets, which would be beneficial for the financing of economic growth and investment and mobilization of savings. At present, government debt is issued in all GCC countries, except the United Arab Emirates, but secondary market turnover is minimal. In addition, the tradable stock of government debt within the region is relatively low (less than 20 percent of GDP), and banks tend to hold securities up to maturity given their excess liquidity and the still limited choice of alternative domestic (regional) investment instruments. Each GCC country has a stock exchange as the trading platform for equities, government securities, and corporate bonds. However, capitalization of most GCC countries' equity markets is still relatively low and turnover minimal.[3] Supervision and regulation of capital markets also exhibit weaknesses that authorities have only just begun to address. With the exception of Oman, the other GCC countries had until recently very restrictive rules for foreign investors in their stock markets. Qatar still does not allow nonnationals to buy stocks and securities (ex-

cept for two listed companies), while in some other GCC countries, foreigners can invest only through open-ended mutual funds.

Measures conducive to market development and integration that should accompany a monetary union include harmonizing national taxes, legislation,[4] and accounting rules related to the holding and trading of securities, while putting in place integrated securities settlement systems. The latter are important to ensure that trades are secure and can be carried out at low transaction costs within the region. Economies of scale could be captured by linking or consolidating stock exchanges, in particular given the limited size of each national market; such a trend can also be observed internationally. Experience with the EMU shows that the introduction of the euro has fostered the integration and development of deeper and more liquid Euro-bond and equity markets, but it has not eliminated all barriers to market integration. The sources for the remaining market fragmentation are differences in tax, accounting, and legal frameworks, and lack of fully integrated clearing and settlement systems. Deficiencies in all those aspects together with the small size of the markets have kept bond and equity markets in the ECCU and CFA zones fragmented and undeveloped.

Integration of the Banking System

Whether a monetary union can contribute to stimulating cross-border banking operations depends foremost on the degree to which the region's banking systems will be liberalized, and legislative, regulatory, and supervisory frameworks harmonized. The banking systems in the GCC countries are already well developed and capitalized, as well as profitable, and have become a major factor in diversifying the production base in some countries, particularly in Bahrain (Table 4.3). Most GCC countries have, however, refrained from licensing any new banks since the early 1980s. Moreover, the role of foreign banks is somewhat limited and confined to the smaller GCC members, where about half of the credit institutions are foreign owned, but account for a smaller percent of banks' assets, except in Bahrain.[5] Only a few local banks have established branches in other GCC countries—though they have branches in other countries in the region and in Asia.[6]

---

[3]Except the stock market of Saudi Arabia, which with a market capitalization of more than 40 percent of GDP, is by far the largest in the region and Arab world.

[4]For example, limits on foreign ownership of stocks, either by law or under the companies' articles of association.

[5]In addition to the onshore markets, Bahrain has developed into an offshore banking center with close to 50 offshore banks.

[6]Two U.A.E. banks have branches in Bahrain, Oman, and Qatar, and one bank has branches in Bahrain and Kuwait. One Omani bank has a branch in the United Arab Emirates and recently bought an existing bank in Bahrain.

Table 4.3. GCC Countries: Selected Financial Sector Indicators[1]

	Bahrain	Kuwait	Oman	Qatar	Saudi Arabia	United Arab Emirates
Total number of banks	22	10	17	15	11	46
Public banks	2 (specialized banks).	Government owns minority shares in several banks.	2 (specialized banks).	1	0	0
Mixed-capital banks	5	8	1 (government owns part of one national bank).	1	1 (government owns 40 percent).	5
Private domestic banks	2	1	4	6	9 (7 joint ventures with foreign banks).	15
Foreign banks	13	1	9	7	1 (branch of a GCC bank).	26
Other credit institutions	0	0	1 specialized private bank.	0	4 specialized credit institutions.	0
Asset quality						
Nonperforming loan ratio	13.1 percent[2]	5.2 percent	11.3 percent	10.7 percent	9.6 percent	11.2 percent
Credit to the public sector/total credit	20 percent	45 percent	12 percent	38 percent	30 percent	10 percent
Credit to the private sector/total credit	80 percent	55 percent	88 percent	62 percent	70 percent	90 percent
Of which: personal credit	36 percent	18 percent	35 percent	33 percent	22 percent	25 percent (includes "for business purposes").
Earnings and profitability						
Return on assets	1.6 percent	2 percent	0.1 percent	2 percent	1.8 percent	1.7 percent
Return on equity	12 percent	18 percent	1.2 percent	17.1 percent	30.8 percent	14.6 percent
Liquidity						
Loans to deposit ratio	63 percent	68 percent	82.1 percent	80 percent	69 percent	92 percent
Domestic government securities						
Held by local banks (in percent of GDP)	...	...	6.2 percent	11.3 percent (1999).	17.3 percent	No government securities issued.
Stock market						
Capitalization (in billions of U.S. dollars)	6.6	18.9	3.6	5.3	74.0	13.5
Number of companies listed	42	91	45 (regular market).	22	76	12 (in Dubai); 15 (in Abu Dhabi).
Deposit insurance	Implicit.	Implicit.	Explicit (established in 1995).	Implicit.	Implicit.	Implicit.

Source: National authorities.
[1]Latest available information.
[2]Does not cover the loans of two Islamic banks.

In a GCC monetary union, some consolidation of the banking systems might take place. The potential impact of a monetary union on the growth of bank loans and the type or structure of banking activities is, however, indirect. Whether overall lending increases is mostly a question of economic growth and new investment opportunities in the region. Greater competition for borrowers is more likely to have an effect on credit conditions than on the overall lending level. Diversifying the credit portfolio could be beneficial for banks' risk management since in several GCC countries bank credit is concentrated in consumer loans. The overall development and integration of financial markets could affect the type of bank operations.[7]

Potential Costs of a Monetary Union

Having operated under a pegged exchange rate regime and liberal capital flows, the GCC countries have de facto refrained from using national monetary and exchange rate policies for more than two decades. Nevertheless, since in the long term, the importance of oil production is likely to diverge among the GCC countries, relinquishing these policies could be costlier in the long run. Thus, a higher degree of domestic labor flexibility and flexible fiscal policies would then be needed to facilitate adjustments to external shocks. Moreover, an important cost factor or risk for a monetary union could arise from negative externalities from the lack of fiscal prudence in one or more member countries. As a result, negative spillover effects could spread from one member country to the entire membership, with the potential need of the union's central bank to raise interest rates particularly in the case of an exchange rate peg of the common currency. A key challenge is therefore to set up rules, penalties, and institutional procedures to prevent major macroeconomic imbalances and lack of fiscal discipline in the monetary union. Rigorous macroeconomic policymaking would not only be an outcome of a monetary union but is an essential condition for its functioning (see Section V for more details).

Cost of Institutional Changes

Replacing the existing national currencies by a common currency involves changeover costs. One-time costs are related, for example, to the conversion of accounts and means of book-money payments (checks, transfer forms, cards), price lists and catalogues, adjustment of cashiers and automats, and educating the public about the new currency—the introduction of the euro is estimated to have cost about 0.5 percent of the euro area GDP.

Creating a new monetary institution initially also requires additional resources. There is room for overall savings if central bank functions are organized more efficiently, and duplication of functions at the national and regional level is avoided.[8] While a monetary union requires a centralized decision-making body for the entire region, other key functions can be allocated at either the national or regional level. As discussed in Section V, practical and political considerations, including cost efficiency considerations, suggest that national central banks could maintain the functions of implementing regular monetary policy and foreign exchange operations, supervising banks, and collecting data. A common GCC central bank or supranational monetary authority would then be in charge of policy decision making, communicating the policy with the public, consolidating financial data at the regional level, and coordinating issues of regional importance. Overseeing and operating the payment systems could either be done at the centralized or decentralized level. Other potential costs for members of a GCC currency union could result from potentially lower central bank profits and negative spillovers from a financial crisis. However, both can be limited by appropriate institutional arrangements.

Credit Policies

Retaining national credit policies in a monetary union could impede the effectiveness of monetary policy for the region as a whole as well as the development and integration of securities markets. The importance of credit policies varies among GCC countries. These policies generally aim at stimulating investment in certain sectors, and they are also a tool for the authorities to distribute the proceeds from the oil wealth to its residents. The governments in GCC countries, directly or through specialized credit institutions or development banks, provide soft long-term funding or grants for investment projects, including housing.

---

[7]In the euro area, some changes in the structure of the banking system have taken place since the introduction of a single currency. The trend toward consolidation has been mostly among domestic banks. Despite the intention of some large European banks to merge, national political interests have prevented a stronger cross-border consolidation. Banking systems in the other monetary unions continue to be not well integrated even after the introduction of a common currency a long time ago.

[8]The costs for operating the European Central Bank, measured as expenditure for staff, administration, and depreciation of fixed assets, amounted to 0.0025 percent of GDP on average for 1999 and 2000. At the same time, most national central banks of the European System of Central Banks have begun to streamline their organization and reduce the number of staff.

The government's involvement in credit allocation and funding has two side effects that create negative externalities for other monetary union members. First, the credit channel is disrupted, since the favored sectors are far less responsive to interest rate changes. This limits the effectiveness of monetary policy for the union. Interest rate changes will be felt and transmitted more strongly to the real economy in countries where the government's involvement in credit allocation and funding plays a smaller role. And second, the government's involvement in credit allocation and funding dis-

courages other forms of long-term financing, such as the issuance of securities and the development of securities markets, thus reducing a potential benefit for monetary union. In essence, GCC countries have to decide whether they want to create a level playing field among their economies with the objective of fostering competition and integration by liberalizing credit policies, or they are willing to tolerate distortions created by subsidized (long-term) interest rates with the negative implications for monetary policy effectiveness and overall capital market development.

V Options for Implementing a Monetary Union Among GCC Countries

Ugo Fasano and Andrea Schaechter

As discussed earlier, the GCC countries already have in place important elements to become a successful monetary union. These include labor flexibility owing to unhindered access to expatriate workers at market-determined wages and current and capital account convertibility. In addition, these countries have had for several decades stable nominal bilateral exchange rates and similar nominal interest rates. However, they still must make fundamental choices and take important steps to design and implement an effective monetary union. These steps include the following.

- Maintaining a sustainable fiscal position in all member countries based on a medium-term framework under the same conservative global crude oil price assumption across GCC countries.

- Adopting a common code of fiscal conduct—consisting of fiscal convergence criteria, a common accounting framework for public accounts, and adequate budgetary procedures.

- Establishing adequate data quality, common standards, and timely dissemination of information to assess progress toward convergence criteria and adherence to policy objectives.

- Developing a common exchange rate policy, including pooling of international reserves.

- Designing the institutions, such as a common central bank, to support the monetary union, as well as a common set of monetary policy instruments to ensure that monetary policy operations are effective throughout the union.

While the above steps must be taken before the introduction of the common currency, the pace of structural reforms that complement the monetary union will determine how fast the GCC countries consolidate the economic union and enhance the net benefits of a single currency. In particular, GCC countries should harmonize and coordinate policies to foster the integration and development of financial markets, and improve resource allocation and mobility of production factors, as well as reform the welfare and incentive systems in place to reduce waste and address expenditure rigidities. In addition, member countries should consider adopting a common strategy for foreign ownership to facilitate and broaden investment opportunities in the GCC area. To this end, they should consider establishing a level playing field for both domestic and foreign investors, eliminating discriminatory tax and regulatory practices, providing legal guarantees and equal property rights, and developing well-functioning, open, and integrated equity and financial markets.

Maintaining a Sustainable Fiscal Position

Maintaining a sustainable fiscal position is crucial for the success of the monetary union. Indeed, an unsustainable position, particularly in a major member country, could lead to an overall undesirable policy mix for the union, undermining other key macroeconomic policy objectives, such as price stability, and negatively affecting the creditworthiness of the union as a whole. In addition, in the case of GCC countries, a strong fiscal position is also required to support the exchange rate peg chosen for the common currency.[1]

To maintain a strong fiscal position, GCC countries should consider casting fiscal policy in a medium-term framework. Assuming the same conservative long-run global crude oil price across the GCC area, this implies that GCC governments should make every effort to generate fiscal surpluses in years when positive shocks occur (i.e., actual oil prices above the conservative oil price assumption), and use them to dampen the restrictive effects of periods of negative shocks. As a result, expenditures are likely to be less driven by short-term oil revenue

---

[1]Although, in principle, all national policies generating cross-border spillovers could be subject to some degree of regional policy coordination among members of a monetary union, the merits and costs of fiscal coordination remains highly debatable, see Beetsma and others (2001).

Box 5.1. Fiscal Sustainability and Intergenerational Economic Equity

In countries in which their wealth is derived from nonrenewable resources, such as oil and gas, the assessment of fiscal sustainability must take account of the depletion of this wealth to ensure intergenerational economic equity. Fiscal policymakers in oil-dependent countries must therefore decide how much oil income to spend on the present generation and how much to save for future generations. One way to determine a sustainable level of government consumption out of oil resources is to derive a notional income stream from the stock of government wealth, determined by the present value of expected future government oil revenue. This notional income represents the "permanent income" that can be consumed indefinitely without increasing the government sector's debt and depleting the country's resources, including financial assets.[1]

Several criteria may be applied to determine the permanent income. Two reasonable ones are to maintain the same oil wealth in per capita terms or real terms. The first alternative implies that the government provides a time invariant level of public goods to all citizens over time, which means that the level of government consumption must be restricted today to provide the same benefits across generations. The second criterion is less restrictive, since it implies that the government can consume relatively more today based on the full return of its wealth. The government's actual consumption out of oil wealth can be proxied by the non-oil fiscal balance (defined as total expenditure minus non-oil revenue, including investment income and the depreciation of the government's capital stock).

Estimates of the permanent income rely on several assumptions, including, in particular, the long-run crude oil price, proven oil reserves, and oil output. Because of the uncertainty in estimating these factors, there may be a need for precautionary savings over and above the level implied by the permanent income.[2]

---

[1]For a further analysis of fiscal policy in oil-producing countries, see Engel and Valdes (2000), Barnett and Ossowski (2002), and Fasano (2003).

[2]For instance, if long-term global crude oil prices were to decline to about $21 a barrel, the GCC countries, with the probable exception of Kuwait and Qatar, will likely need to reassess their current level of non-oil fiscal deficit to maintain fiscal sustainability, and avoid increases in debt or drawdowns of government foreign assets over time.

---

availability, limiting the effects of volatile oil prices on the economy. Moreover, this approach will also address the need to ensure a balanced distribution of the oil wealth across generations (intergenerational economic equity) (Box 5.1).

Fiscal Code of Conduct

Given the GCC countries' dependence on volatile oil revenue and the importance of achieving intergenerational economic equity, the choice of fiscal convergence criteria is complex. Several fiscal convergence criteria that complement each other should be considered:[2]

---

[2]For example, budgetary convergence criteria in the West African Economic and Monetary Union (WAEMU) are assessed through the concept of basic fiscal balance—defined as fiscal revenue minus expenditure and excluding both grants and foreign-financed investment. This balance has to be positive or nil. The European Union (EU) uses the concept of overall fiscal balance and the convergence criteria specify a budget deficit of no more than 3 percent of GDP. The coverage of fiscal accounts is also different. The EU's fiscal targets cover the general government, which includes social security and local government accounts, whereas the WAEMU fiscal criteria essentially look at central government finances. Both zones set a ceiling on the overall ratio of public debt to GDP, though in the WAEMU, that ceiling is set at 70 percent as a norm, whereas the EU has a 60 percent target.

- Adopting an overall balanced budget target based on a similar conservative crude oil price assumptions across the GCC area, with actual deficits or surpluses resulting only from terms of trade fluctuations.

- Establishing targets for closely monitoring member countries' non-oil fiscal deficits. However, the non-oil fiscal deficit should not be the same for each country mainly because of different endowment of hydrocarbon and financial wealth. Thus, each GCC country will face a different but sustainable level of government consumption out of this wealth (see Box 5.1).

- Setting a ceiling on total government debt—possibly net of certain liquid government assets. This ceiling would ensure that member countries could not run actual overall deficits for many years in succession, jeopardizing the credibility of the pegged exchange rate regime.

Given the volatility in oil prices and, in turn, nominal GDP, GCC countries should consider alternative options to measure the aforementioned criteria. These could be measured in percent of non-oil GDP or in a common currency. Regarding the coverage of the fiscal accounts, GCC countries should probably look at a broad concept of government, including central and local governments, extrabudgetary government funds, and pension funds. In addition, sound budgetary practices should be followed in order to maintain fiscal sustainability within the union. These practices include, among others, adoption of internationally accepted standards and codes on classification of expenditures and revenues, transparent recording of all revenues and expenditures, and the extent to which the budget is based on a realistic medium-term macroeconomic framework.

It would also be important that all GCC countries mobilize non-oil revenues and improve the structure of public expenditure, so that convergence criteria can be implemented without undue dislocation. The mobilization of non-oil revenues should contribute to broadening the revenue base and making the budget more resilient to oil shocks, while providing room for a more flexible fiscal policy. The structure of fees and charges—the main source of non-oil revenue in the GCC countries—should aim at reducing explicit and implicit budgetary subsidies and establishing proper incentives for private producers to enter the sector and consumers to reduce excessive consumption. For GCC countries with large government debt, privatization receipts could be used to retire the most onerous part of their debt. Moreover, subsidies, particularly to the agricultural and energy sectors, should be phased out, and nonproductive expenditure cut. This move would give room to restructure the budget toward more growth-oriented spending, such as education, health, infrastructure, and other development outlays.

Exchange Rate Arrangement

The pegged exchange rate regime in the GCC countries has contributed over the past decades to anchoring stability, keeping inflation low, and strengthening confidence. These countries have also decided to peg their future common currency to the U.S. dollar. However, other options for the exchange rate regime of the common currency should be considered, including pegging to a basket of currencies, or other more flexible arrangements.[3] Each option clearly carries its own policy implications and operational requirements.

These options should take into account the changing trade patterns over the medium-to-long term—with Europe probably gaining in importance through negotiations under way for a trade agreement between the two areas—and emerging changes in the structure of GCC economies and export composition. Indeed, the weight of the manufacturing sector has been growing very rapidly in Saudi Arabia, as has entrepôt trade and related activities in the United Arab Emirates, while the banking and insurance sector is by far the single most important sector in Bahrain's economy. In Qatar, natural gas is well on the road to bypass oil as the key sector in the economy. Oman has just started to benefit from its growth strategy centered on developing its natural gas resources and tourism. In any case, the exchange rate regime must be supported by a strong fiscal position and a sound banking system. In addition, it must be complemented by structural reforms and human capital development to boost the economy's flexibility, particularly the labor market for nationals, in order to enhance growth prospects for non-oil activities (see below).

The introduction of the monetary union among GCC countries will be marked by irrevocably fixing their bilateral exchange rates. As a result, the national currencies become subunits of the common currency—even before the new common currency replaces national notes and coins in circulation. At the same time, the area's liquidity management becomes the responsibility of the common central bank or supranational monetary authority. In addition, in light of the decision to peg the common currency to the U.S. dollar, GCC countries will have to set the initial exchange rate between both currencies. Given that they already operate under a U.S. dollar peg, the natural choice for the bilateral conversion rates among them are the cross rates based on the mid points at which the GCC central banks stand ready to buy and sell U.S. dollars.[4] The timing for introducing notes and coins of the common currency should depend mostly on the technical preparedness of the region. However, a lesson from the euro experience is that the period in which the national and the common currencies circulate in parallel should be kept short. Requiring businesses to deal simultaneously with two different currencies involves substantial costs—the euro became the sole legal tender two months after its introduction.[5] Of a more political nature is the issue of how a GCC member's individual international reserves should be pooled. The union will need to decide whether the members should make avail-

---

[3]Abed, Erbas, and Guerami (2003) compare the dollar peg to a dollar-euro basket peg as alternative exchange rate regimes for a GCC monetary union. They find that a basket peg does not dominate a dollar peg for improving external stability.

[4]For the introduction of the euro, the bilateral exchange rates were locked in at the bilateral central rates of the exchange rate mechanism, which were announced seven months before the monetary union came into effect.

[5]However, credit institutions have continued to exchange national banknotes and coins for euro for a while, but not always free of charge. National central banks, on the other hand, continue to exchange their respective national banknotes and coins at face value and free of charge for a longer period, though it varies country by country.

able all their official foreign assets for the common exchange rate policy or just a portion.[6]

Institutional Considerations

The creation of a common independent central bank (or unified supranational monetary authority) would be the most important institutional change on the road toward a monetary union. However, institutional and legal frameworks for conducting a single monetary policy also need to be developed to ensure a smooth functioning of a GCC monetary union. The necessary institutional changes could be implemented on a step-by-step basis during the transition period to the introduction of a common currency. This approach has the key advantage of giving market participants and the authorities the opportunity to gradually adjust and become familiar with the changes taking place during the period. For example, in the case of the EMU, the harmonization of most institutional aspects was achieved in stages before the introduction of the euro, including adjustments in national central bank laws (explicitly prohibiting central bank financing of government deficits and strengthening the independence of the national central banks). By contrast, the use of monetary policy instruments continued to vary among the member countries until the EMU came into effect.[7]

A Common Independent Central Bank

From a practical and political perspective, it appears that a decentralized approach to organizing central bank responsibilities, like that of the EMU, will likely be appropriate in the GCC context.[8] The common central bank would be in charge of taking monetary policy decisions, analyzing union-wide economic and financial data, as well as communicating with the public on monetary policy decisions and economic developments in the GCC area. Moreover, the common central bank would ensure the operations of effectively linked payment systems to foster the integration of interbank money markets and the effectiveness of monetary policy. Guiding and coordinating initiatives for better regional financial market integration and development would mostly relate to harmonizing financial regulations and procedures.[9]

Under such a decentralized approach, the national GCC central banks would implement the monetary policy decisions and conduct all or some of the foreign exchange operations, maintain their banking supervisory functions, issue the common currency, and operate the national payment systems.[10] Based on their experience and their institutional knowledge, the GCC central banks currently have a comparative advantage of carrying out banking supervision over a newly created regional institution.[11] In this function, they would also collect national bank data, which would then be consolidated by the common central bank.[12] With banking supervision and bank data collection remaining with the national central banks, it would then be advantageous to implement monetary policy decisions at the national level since the information gained through the close contact between national central banks and commercial banks can also be useful for the supervisory function. In the long run however, with more integrated banking systems and financial markets, and if there is political consensus, it could become more efficient to shift the responsibilities for banking super-

---

[6]The ECCU and the CFA zones are both monetary unions that operate under a fixed exchange rate for the common currency. In the ECCU, all reserves are pooled with the ECCB. In the CFA zone, the national central banks have to deposit 65 percent of their foreign reserves at an operations account with the French treasury. Each CFA country draws down on its own account of pooled and unpooled reserves whenever necessary. Once these reserves are fully drawn down, the other member countries' pooled reserves may be used. By contrast, for the euro area, the impact of the common exchange rate policy on foreign reserves has not been a particular issue because the euro floats freely. However, interventions can be conducted by the ECB and the national European central banks (on request of the ECB). The member countries have transferred a predefined amount of foreign reserves to the ECB, and the latter can make further calls on the national central banks' foreign reserves under certain conditions.

[7]Creating a GCC monetary institute, similar to the European Monetary Institute, could facilitate the transition period by identifying the required adjustments, recommending policy options, and developing the operational framework, as well as laying the technical and organizational foundations needed.

[8]The "euro system" is composed of the ECB and the national central banks, which are largely independent of national governments.

[9]In a monetary union, three types of institutions could carry out all or some of a central bank's functions: first, a common, newly established central bank (or unified monetary authority); second, the existing national central banks; and third, one of the member's central bank. Although for all of the three options some form of "branch network" would have to be maintained, the degree of responsibilities allocated to the branches would differ.

[10]In the EMU, the issuance of the common currency in circulation is determined by each national central bank based on cash demand.

[11]While banking supervision has traditionally been a central bank responsibility, it can also be allocated to another national or supranational public entity, as for instance, in the United Kingdom.

[12]This consolidation would also require that bank returns be harmonized among GCC countries.

vision and monetary policy operations to the regional level.

This proposed setup would require a central decision-making body for monetary policy. This body could be formed by all six GCC central bank governors appointed at the national level, together with the executives of the common central bank appointed at the regional level.[13] Also, the common central bank should be granted operational independence; that is, it should be given the discretion to set its monetary instruments according to its policy objectives without direct or indirect political interference. Accordingly, the national central bank laws would have to be revised.

The contribution of each GCC member country to the capital and seigniorage distribution of a common central bank would also have to be considered for the monetary union. There are several ways to determine the individual country's contribution to the capital base of the common central bank. Typically, the economic strength or the size of a country is considered and measured, for instance, by its share in the union's GDP and population. The overall level of capital has to be sufficient for the common central bank to fulfill its responsibilities. The central bank law should provide for further capital injections by the members when central bank losses erode the capital base.

As regards seigniorage, there will be winners and losers in the monetary union depending on the rules for its distribution. A country will lose seigniorage in a monetary union if its share in the common central bank's profits is lower than its share in the aggregate monetary base. For example, in the euro area, seigniorage is distributed according to the shares in capital. Germany has been identified as a net loser of seigniorage because its share in the aggregate monetary base was about 35 percent, but its equity share amounted to only about 25 percent.

Monetary Policy Instruments

To ensure that monetary policy operations have the desired effects throughout the monetary union, the common central bank and the national central banks must possess a common set of monetary policy instruments. While the common central bank would define the conditions of the policy instruments, the national central banks would apply them, purely as agents of the common central bank.[14] For example, the mechanism and characteristics of any loan and deposit operations have to be the same in all member countries. If interest rates are set by the common central bank, they should apply to all member countries. If these operations are the outcome of an auction procedure, the results should be determined by the overall bids and not country by country. Similarly, all characteristics of reserve requirements, such as the reserve ratio, the reserve base, remuneration rate, and sanctions, would have to be identical throughout the region. Moreover, to create a level playing field, all central bank counterparties have to be informed simultaneously about upcoming monetary operations and face the same deadlines and other conditions to submit their bids.[15]

In general, the common policy instruments should allow conducting monetary policy efficiently, in a simple and transparent manner, conforming to market principles, and contributing to financial market development. One important issue to be addressed by the GCC countries in preparation for a monetary union is the choice of assets for collateral. Since GCC countries' government securities are only held by some banks in the region, and secondary markets do not yet function efficiently, consideration must be given to what other assets (e.g., sovereign papers issued outside the GCC area) to allow and what risk control measures to apply.

Financial Crisis Management

Financial crisis management in a GCC monetary union will need to be designed to avoid a conflict between any liquidity support provided to distressed commercial banks and the regional monetary policy

---

[13]The decision-making body of the ECB consists of the 12 governors of the national central banks and the six members of the ECB's executive board. In the monetary unions in Africa, in the BCEAO, the Board of Directors consists of two directors per country and the BCEAO governor, who cannot vote in decisions. The number of country representatives in the Board of Directors of the BEAC varies according to the size of the economy (with four directors from Cameroon, two from Gabon, and one from each of the other members; France also sends three directors).

[14]Nevertheless, the monetary union might find itself in a situation in which it has to react quickly to shocks. Thus, the common central bank should have the authority and technical framework to conduct short-term monetary and foreign exchange operations in case the organization of the operations through the national central banks is too slow.

[15]Small technical differences can be warranted to accommodate national differences, particularly regarding collateral assets. For example, in the euro area, the main policy instruments are refinancing operations, which can be conducted either as repurchase transactions or as collateralized loans reflecting differences in country experiences and legal treatments of the operations. The set of eligible assets for collateral consists of two tiers. Tier one assets are set by the ECB, while tier two assets (of particular importance for some countries, such as bills of exchange) are listed by the national central banks on approval by the ECB.

stance.[16] Similar to the discussion above on fiscal rules, the objective of a crisis management mechanism would be to contain negative externalities. A cornerstone for the financial stability of the region is to further strengthen banking supervision in each member country—a high degree of compliance with Basel Core Principles has already been achieved in most GCC countries. As long as banking supervision remains a national task, the responsibilities for crisis management and resolution, including emergency liquidity support, would also be appropriately set at the country level, so that costs and risks of providing financial assistance would be borne at the level at which they occur. Nevertheless, timely communication with the common central bank and other national central banks is crucial to limit negative spillovers through the overall liquidity impact and any other cross-border effects. In the long-run, when institutional capacity has been built and financial markets have become more integrated, it might be beneficial to centralize the function of banking supervision and crisis management. The allocation of responsibilities among all relevant parties, including ministries of finance, other financial sector supervisors, and deposit insurance agencies, powers, and the procedures for crisis management and resolution will need to be explicitly laid out in advance to ensure smooth and quick responses to crisis situations.

As an example, the euro area countries have put in place a decentralized crisis management mechanism. This mechanism has not been tested yet, though it has been at the center of many discussions on the feasibility and desirability of decentralized banking supervision and crisis management in a monetary union. The main three characteristics of the process are as follows. First, crisis management is decentralized. The EMU members are primarily responsible for providing emergency liquidity assistance and shouldering the associated costs and risks. Second, the national central banks have to ensure an adequate flow of information with the ECB, so that overall

liquidity can be managed consistently with the monetary policy stance. And third, no explicit rules are spelled out in advance to determine under which conditions the EMU members should give liquidity support to commercial banks. This approach of "constructive ambiguity" is supposed to limit the potential adverse consequences of moral hazard.

Data Standards and Transparency

Assessing the success of convergence and adherence to policy objectives will require comparable, transparent macroeconomic and financial statistical information among GCC countries. Public availability of this information and their timeliness would greatly enhance regional surveillance, help implement appropriate economic policies, and very possibly limit excessive macroeconomic divergence across GCC countries.[17] In particular, comparable fiscal concepts, methods, and data should be readily available to policymakers. For monetary policy decisions, the common central bank will also have to rely on a set of harmonized statistics. To construct a consolidated balance sheet of the national central banks, the common central bank, and commercial banks, accounting rules and standards will also have to be harmonized. It would be useful to create an independent regional statistical office in charge of developing concepts and methods and providing the consolidated and harmonized GCC level data that are collected by the national authorities.[18]

Structural Reforms

Although structural reforms are desirable independent of the introduction of a monetary union, they are likely to enhance the positive effects of the common currency. Thus, the GCC countries should give priority to improving resource allocation and mobility of production factors and to promoting foreign direct investment. To deepen financial markets, a GCC monetary union will need to be comple-

---

[16]In the GCC area, over the past two decades, Kuwait twice experienced a systemic bank failure: following the crash of the informal stock market in 1982 and the Iraqi invasion in 1990. In the first case, the government recapitalized all but one bank, and bought shares of several banks, becoming minority owner of three and majority holder of four. In the second crisis, the government purchased from the banks most of their delinquent debt portfolios with government bonds. The United Arab Emirates has also successfully resolved several bank failures through the merger of banks; liquidation; recapitalization by existing shareholders, new shareholders, or a public entity; and/or liquidity support from the central bank. In Oman, the government recapitalized one bank affected by the collapse of the Bank of Credit and Commerce International in 1991. In Qatar, the central bank intervened and recapitalized in 2002, a commercial bank affected by the collapse of a large private local industrial group.

---

[17]Most GCC countries currently issue a Public Information Notice after the IMF Executive Board's conclusion of Article IV consultations. Some of them have also started to publish their consultation reports on the IMF's public website.

[18]The experience of the EU in this area could be instructive. The Statistical Office of the European Communities (Eurostat)—created in 1953—has gained importance with the preparation for the EMU, and is now the only provider of statistics at the European level. The EMU has fueled the concept of harmonizing methodologies between member states, which adopted several laws in that respect. Today, many economic indicators are harmonized, including the CPI, GDP, and fiscal balances.

mented by a number of regulatory and legislative adjustments designed to liberalize national financial markets and foster harmonization.

Financial Integration

With private securities markets still nascent and equity markets relatively small and underdeveloped in most GCC countries, several measures should be adopted to further foster the integration and development of these markets in the GCC area. These include the harmonization of national capital taxation, legislation (e.g., limits on foreign ownership of stocks), and accounting related to the holding and trading of securities and equities. In addition, the GCC authorities should address remaining weaknesses in the supervision and regulation of securities markets as well as corporate governance issues. The harmonization and coordination of rules for foreign investors in the stock market could also encourage portfolio investment in the area.

To further integrate the banking system in the GCC area, the authorities should facilitate the cross-border banking consolidation that will likely take place in a monetary union. Increased cross-border banking operations are likely to depend on the degree to which the region's banking systems are liberalized and the legislative, regulatory, and supervisory frameworks harmonized.

Labor Market

The labor market in the GCC area is segmented between expatriate and national workers in terms of skills, wages, nonwage benefits, and sectors of employment. In a monetary union with a pegged exchange rate regime, the cost of jobs losses in the face of external shocks could be higher. Given that all GCC countries have taken steps to reduce the share of expatriate labor in the total labor force, these countries should also aim at the same time to achieve a flexible labor market for nationals, and reduce labor segmentation. To this end, these countries should diminish disparities in incentives between public and private sectors to encourage nationals to seek employment in the private sector at internationally competitive wages.[19]

GCC countries should also apply with pragmatism and flexibility employment targets for nationals (quotas), ensuring that employers have sufficient maneu-

verability to hire the most qualified labor—at market-determined wages to maintain competitiveness, particularly in the non-oil sector. Concurrently, education and training programs should be further reinforced and upgraded to provide nationals with the appropriate skills and productivity performance to enhance their employability as economic diversification takes place. Moreover, all GCC countries could consider introducing an unemployment insurance scheme and extending pension benefits to nationals working in the private sector.

Measures should be also adopted to encourage cross-border labor mobility of GCC nationals. These could include transferable social insurance systems, the harmonization of nonwage benefits across countries—probably financed by a pool of resources among GCC countries—and mutual recognition of qualifications at all levels through the adoption of joint GCC educational curricula. In addition, a common housing policy could be adopted, where GCC nationals could receive current benefits related to the sharing of the oil wealth of their respective country independently of where they live or work in the GCC area.

Other Structural Reforms

In addition to the structural reforms mentioned above, other structural reforms could also complement the monetary union among GCC countries. Economic and monetary integration can be considered credible (and sustainable over time) only if the member states maintain a sufficient level of economic and social cohesion to lessen the gaps in development and living standards across the membership.[20] Thus, differences in welfare and incentive systems, commercial laws and codes, and regulations of businesses and commercial agencies must be reduced significantly in the coming years. Agreements to enlarge the domestic market and facilitate inward investment through the harmonization and coordination of tax, legal, and pensions systems, as well as the elimination of nontariff barriers to intra-GCC investment should also be reached. Rules and incentives governing foreign investment and the regional market should be harmonized to facilitate an efficient movement of capital among member countries. Moreover, the judicial system must be modernized in all GCC countries, including the adoption of bankruptcy laws. Thus, these reforms should be coordinated on a GCC-wide basis to

---

[19]For several decades, the EU has had a European Social Fund (ESF) to promote employment and encourage worker mobility. The ESF has become the EU's primary social policy instrument, and currently funds training, vocational retraining, and job creation measures to improve the way labor markets operate and to get the unemployed back into jobs.

[20]The EU established Structural Funds to promote economic development, including of human resources, and structural adjustment of regions whose performances are lagging behind (as indicated by an average per capita GDP 75 percent below the EU average). The annual funding for these funds reached on average about 0.50 percent of the EU's GNP during the 1990s.

contribute to an "open integration" strategy and reduce distortions, implying that regional integration should be a mean to attain greater efficiency and enhance competitiveness.

Despite diversification efforts in most GCC countries, the role of the private sector remains limited in both the oil and non-oil sectors. Governments continue to engage in commercial activities and the delivery of a wide range of services, usually priced at subsidized rates. Disengagement from these activities through privatization and build-operate-transfer schemes—as is currently the case in the power and water sector in most GCC countries—would contribute not only to permanent and significant expenditure savings, but also to a better allocation of resources, enhancing the potential benefits of a common currency. The increases in utility tariffs could be phased in over time. Full cost recovery pricing of power, water, and other services, such as health, would require the adoption of targeted subsidies and the setting up of a compensatory mecha-

nism to protect low-income groups or the most vulnerable sectors of society.

Although taxes are currently not a major source of government revenues in the GCC area, there is a strong case for their harmonization or coordination based on allocative efficiency and welfare enhancement. In a monetary union, companies will likely pay more attention to differences in the costs of doing business in different member countries, while individuals would move where taxes are lower (and services better or cheaper). Thus, in the absence of coordination, taxes on mobile factors could end up being inefficiently low, and taxes on less mobile factors inefficiently high.[21]

---

[21]In Europe, the Maastricht Treaty had no implications for the harmonization of tax structures and welfare programs, while value-added tax rates still vary widely across countries, and neither rates nor exemptions have converged much. It seems that noncurrency factors, such as transportation cost of cross-border shopping, have ensured that such differences persist so far.

Appendix I   Economic Performance and Policies of GCC Countries, 1990–2002

The GCC countries implemented from 1990 to 2002 a broad range of structural and institutional reforms to accelerate non-oil growth and create employment opportunities for a rapidly rising local labor force, while reducing vulnerability to oil price shocks. These reforms have in common several key elements, such as lifting impediments to foreign direct investment, streamlining business regulations, expanding private sector investment opportunities, improving governance, and modernizing the financial system. GCC countries have also strengthened efforts in the past decade to diversify their production base, including through the development of liquefied natural gas, gas-based industries, and services, such as container port facilities and tourism. This appendix reviews overall economic performance in these countries since 1990, as well as progress in implementing their structural reform agenda, which is being reinforced by ongoing regional economic and monetary integration.

Bahrain

Endowed with smaller oil reserves than its neighbors in the GCC area, Bahrain has promoted over the past decades a number of non-oil based economic activities.[1] These included establishing an export-oriented, gas-based aluminum manufacturing industry, building up an offshore financial center (including Islamic banking), promoting the tourism industry, and, recently, encouraging information-technology industries. As a result, although the Bahraini economy remains dominated by the public sector, it has become the most diversified in the GCC area: the non-oil sector accounts for over 80 percent of real GDP, with the financial sector being the single most important activity in the country (contributing about 20 percent of real GDP).[2]

Supported by a liberal trade and investment regime, no taxation, and minimum business regulations, Bahrain's aggregate real GDP growth averaged about 4.5 percent a year during 1991–2002. This contributed to a gradual improvement in the country's GDP per capita.[3] Also, economic growth has become quite resilient to oil price shocks as reflected in a relatively robust non-oil growth, even in 1998 when global oil prices collapsed. Meanwhile, Bahrain's real effective exchange rate—amid one of the lowest inflation rates in the GCC area (about 0.5 percent a year on average from 1991 to 2002)—has depreciated slightly over the same period, though it has been quite volatile (Table A1.1).

Bahrain's financial position has, however, remained vulnerable to oil price movements, because oil still accounts for over 60 percent of both export receipts and government revenues despite a relatively diversified economic structure. Thus, as a result of the downward trend in global oil prices during much of the last decade through 1998, Bahrain recorded fiscal and external current account deficits—albeit moderate ones. The government financed the fiscal deficits mainly through domestic debt, which increased rapidly—though from a low base. In 2000, strong world prices for key exports commodities (gas, aluminum, and particularly oil) sparked an improved financial performance. Indeed, the fiscal accounts swung into a large surplus (close to 10 percent of GDP)—most of it set aside in the Reserve Fund for Strategic Projects—and the external account balance also switched to a surplus, though one of the

---

This appendix was prepared by Behrouz Guerami (Bahrain), Ibrahim Al Gelaiqah (Kuwait), Van Can Thai (Oman), Bright Okogu (Qatar), Shehadah Hussein (Saudi Arabia), and John Wilson (United Arab Emirates), with contributions from Ugo Fasano.

[1]Onshore proven fossil fuel reserves are expected to be exhausted in about 15 years at the current rate of production. About 80 percent of Bahrain's offshore oil comes from the Abu Saafa oil field in Saudi Arabia, with its proceeds accruing to Bahrain indefinitely.

[2]The public sector dominates about 60 percent of GDP, with the government owning 77 percent of the aluminum industry, the cornerstone of the non-oil sector activity in manufacturing.

[3]Many outside analysts rank Bahrain as the country with the most open economy and strongest social indicators in the Middle East. For instance, on its 2002 index of economic freedom, the Heritage Foundation ranks Bahrain as first in the region and fifteenth worldwide.

Table A1.1. GCC Countries: Real Effective Exchange Rates and Inflation Volatility, 1991–2002

	Real Effective Exchange Rate			CPI-Inflation		
	Average[1]	Standard deviation	Coefficient of variation[2]	Average	Standard deviation	Coefficient of variation[2]
Bahrain	−0.33	4.81	−14.44	0.56	1.39	2.50
Kuwait	1.19	4.31	3.62	1.73	2.60	1.11
Oman	−0.65	4.01	−6.20	0.18	1.74	9.55
Qatar[3]	1.04	4.92	4.72	2.06	2.34	1.13
Saudi Arabia	−0.46	4.34	−9.40	0.64	2.14	2.94
United Arab Emirates	2.18	4.90	2.24	3.53	1.55	0.44

Sources: National authorities; and IMF staff estimates.
[1]A negative sign means that the real effective exchange rate depreciated on average in the period.
[2]Standard deviation divided by mean (average).
[3]Excludes 1996 due to a sharp adjustment in some fees and charges.

lowest in the GCC region (less than 2 percent of GDP). In 2001–02, as a result of weaker crude oil prices, it is estimated that Bahrain recorded a small fiscal surplus (less than 1 percent of GDP on average), while the external current account was practically balanced (Figure A1.1).

Notwithstanding the recent improvement in the overall fiscal accounts, the underlying fiscal position has remained weak. After declining during the first half of the 1990s, the non-oil fiscal deficit deteriorated significantly during the second half, particularly between 1998 and 2002, when it increased by about 60 percent in nominal terms (or from 15 percent to about 21 percent of GDP), reflecting higher current expenditures across the board—Bahrain's wage bill at more than 13 percent of GDP is among the highest in the GCC area. This deterioration took place even though non-oil revenues, in particular fees and charges, increased significantly as the authorities adopted cost recovery measures for government-provided services, such as electricity, water, and sewerage. Moreover, budget policy has usually presented a "stop-and-go" approach. When oil prices fell, capital expenditures have been cut, while current spending, in particular the wage bill, have remained practically untouched.

Bahrain's well-capitalized and supervised financial sector has been quite profitable, with a sound asset quality. The Bahrain Monetary Agency (BMA) maintains a strict segregation between the domestic and the offshore financial systems.[4] Aside from conventional banking, the BMA's recent efforts to develop a comprehensive regulatory and operational framework for Islamic banking has supported the government's ongoing efforts to establish Bahrain as a leading Islamic financial center. The BMA adheres to Basel Core Principles for Effective Banking. Stable and credible monetary and exchange rate policies have also helped maintain a sound financial system.

The BMA is in charge of enforcing monetary policy, which is basically directed at short-term regulation of domestic liquidity by using indirect instruments. It also uses open market operations to manage domestic liquidity by discounting treasury bills and government development bonds, as well as by carrying out foreign exchange swap operations with commercial banks. Monetary policy is framed within a currency board type of arrangement, which maintains foreign exchange coverage of 100 percent of the currency in circulation. The authorities have recently adopted a new law and several regulations to combat money laundering and the financing of terrorism.

Although economic growth has remained buoyant through much of the last decade, unemployment pressures among nationals have started to mount, since the vibrant sectors in the economy (offshore banking, trade, and tourism) continue to depend largely on expatriate workers for employment. To deal with this problem, the Bahraini authorities have adopted an active policy of training and education, flexible employment quotas, and incentives for firms to employ Bahraini nationals.[5] Moreover, they have established recruitment centers to help employers find qualified and suitable local candidates. These measures have had some success in gradually reduc-

---

[4]Offshore banks are not allowed to accept deposits or provide loans to residents, but are permitted to borrow funds from commercial banks on the interbank market.

[5]Expatriate workers account for about 60 percent of the workforce and for about 70 percent of private sector employment.

Figure A1.1. Bahrain and GCC Countries: Selected Economic Indicators[1]

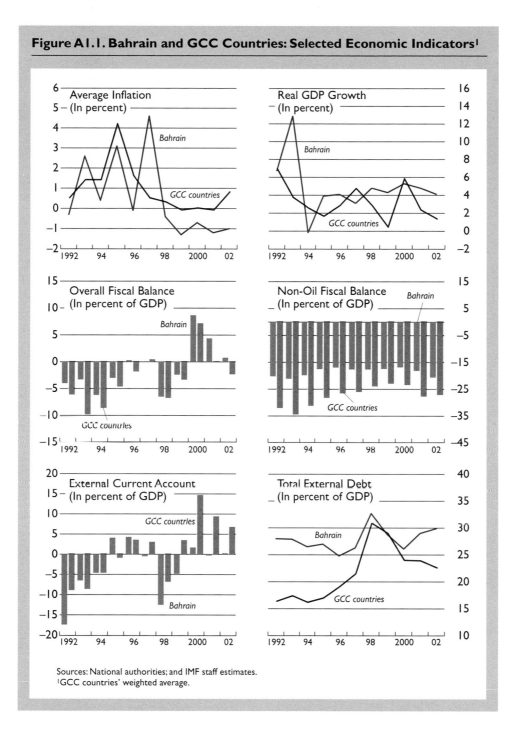

Sources: National authorities; and IMF staff estimates.
[1]GCC countries' weighted average.

ing the share of expatriate workers in the workforce, but a rapidly growing national labor force has hindered further improvement.

Structural reforms have advanced gradually in Bahrain. These reforms have aimed at improving the general functioning of public administration and promoting the role of the private sector. The authorities have completed the public expenditure reviews for

education and health and contracted out the management of two small public enterprises (Appendix III). Progress in privatization has been limited, in part due to the possibility of worsening unemployment among nationals in the short run. The authorities have also simplified administrative procedures and business licensing, and reformed the investment laws to make Bahrain more attractive to foreign direct investment (barriers for non-GCC foreign companies to own real estate have been eased as well).[6] In addition, import tariffs on selected consumer products are in line with the adoption of the GCC common external tariff in January 2003.

Kuwait

During the past decade, Kuwait has made an impressive recovery from the economic damage and disruptions caused by Iraq's invasion in the early 1990s. In fact, oil output capacity and exports have been restored, and the fiscal and external account deficits of the mid-1990s have been eliminated and have turned to surpluses of over 20 percent of GDP in recent years.[7] At the same time, foreign assets and the country's infrastructure have been rebuilt, public debt drastically reduced, and the financial system strengthened. Inflation, which increased sharply in the aftermath of the regional conflict, averaging 10 percent a year in the early 1990s, fell on average to about 2 percent a year in the latter part of the decade through 2002 (Figure A1.2). In addition, the cushion provided by large and rising government investment income receipts has reduced Kuwait's vulnerability to unfavorable developments in international oil markets. Indeed, even in 1998 when global oil prices collapsed, Kuwait and the United Arab Emirates were the only GCC countries to record an external current account surplus.

Following the reconstruction boom, Kuwait's growth in recent years has been weak. Real GDP growth averaged about 1 percent a year from 1996 to 2002, reflecting a drop in oil output. In addition, despite the recovery in non-oil growth (averaging 2 percent over the same period), this sector's share of total GDP remains below that of the 1980s.[8] The government sector continues to dominate most economic activities, including oil, transportation, telecommunications, utilities, and financial services.

Kuwait recorded a strong financial position in the 1990s—except in the early part of the decade, owing to the high spending associated with reconstruction following the end of the regional conflict. The pru-

dent fiscal policy reflects the objective of building up official reserves, so that future generations will benefit from the proceeds of the nonrenewable oil reserves extracted in the current period.[9] The strengthening of the overall fiscal budget position in recent years was greatly assisted by large increases in global crude oil prices, a rapid expansion of income from investments in foreign assets, and higher transfers of profits of public entities. Also, total expenditures were reduced significantly, resulting in a decline in their ratio to GDP from 59 percent in 1993/94 to an average of about 40 percent in 1999/2001—though it has edged up in 2001/02, leading to a deterioration in the non-oil fiscal deficit. Except for wages and salaries, all other spending categories were affected, in particular goods and services, reflecting cutbacks in military outlays. Despite this improvement, the structure of the budget has remained weak, with heavy dependence still remaining on oil revenues, and large outlays related to the costs and subsidies associated with the "cradle to the grave" social welfare system.

A wide array of budgetary subsidies and transfers, both direct and indirect, is provided by the government to the Kuwaiti population. A sharp increase in subsidies and transfers took place in the immediate post-conflict years, owing to payments to Kuwaiti nationals living abroad, and the transfers associated with the government's forgiveness of all consumer and housing loans of Kuwaiti nationals outstanding at the time of the Iraqi invasion. Outlays on subsidies and transfers have since moderated, although they nevertheless have remained high, averaging 9 percent of GDP in the second half of the 1990s. Developments in Kuwait's balance of payments have reflected the economy's heavy dependence on oil exports and investment income, which have accounted for more than 90 percent of all current account receipts. Despite this dependence, the country has traditionally recorded (large) current account surpluses.

Monetary policy in Kuwait has been centered on maintaining price stability, and fostering a sound financial system. The exchange rate arrangement—pegged until recently to an undisclosed basket of currencies of Kuwait's trade and financial partners—has continued to serve the country well, keeping inflation low and enhancing confidence.[10] The policy strategy in recent years has been to

---

[6]The Economic Development Board (established in April 2000) is to recommend and oversee these reforms, acting as the one-stop shop to handle and approve all foreign direct investment applications in the country.

[7]IMF staff estimates of the overall fiscal balance differ from official data because the former include investment income of government foreign assets.

[8]The non-oil sector as a share of GDP fell during 1996–2002 to 52 percent of GDP, relative to an average of 66 percent in the 1980s, while in 2002, the oil sector is estimated to have accounted for more than 48 percent of GDP, 92 percent of exports, and 88 percent of budget revenues.

[9]The policy of reserve accumulation was formalized in 1976, when the government passed a law requiring that 10 percent of all budget revenues be diverted to the Reserve Fund for Future Generations. See Fasano (2000) for further details.

[10]In October 2002, the Kuwaiti authorities announced that they would peg the local currency to the U.S. dollar effective January 2003 in line with the GCC decision to achieve a monetary union by 2010.

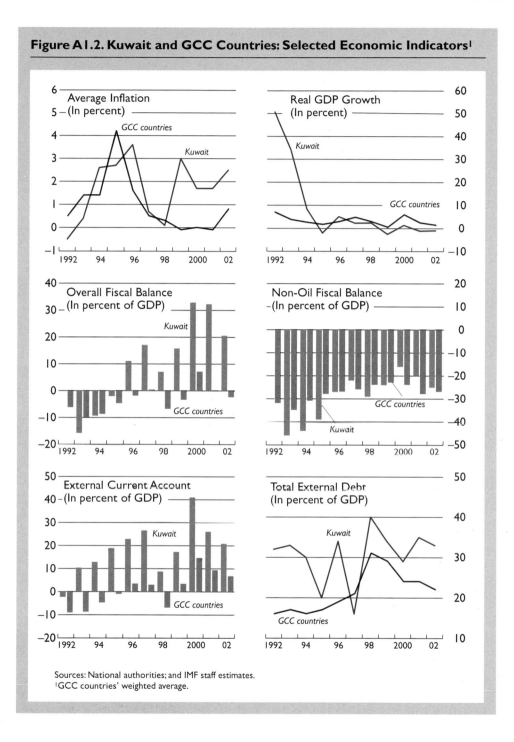

Figure A1.2. Kuwait and GCC Countries: Selected Economic Indicators[1]

Sources: National authorities; and IMF staff estimates.
[1]GCC countries' weighted average.

maintain a foreign reserve target of not less than five months of goods imports, to refrain from central bank financing of the government, and to strengthen prudential regulations in line with international standards. In the last decade, the Central Bank of Kuwait's monetary policy instruments have evolved toward increased reliance on indirect instruments of liquidity management, in line with increasing financial liberalization. All controls on deposit interest and limits on bank charges and fees were abolished in 1995, leaving only controls on maximum rates of bank loans. At present, liquidity management is conducted primarily by means of open market operations, in addition to direct deposit-taking and lending at rates closely guided by market conditions.

In the 1990s, Kuwait's financial system made great strides in recovering from the stresses related to the 1982 crash of the informal stock market, and the impact of Iraq's invasion. In order to tackle these financial problems, the government introduced the Debt Collection Program (DCP) in 1993–94 to restore the integrity of the financial system.[11] Sizable resources formerly invested abroad have been channeled back to the domestic economy to support credit demand arising from the strengthening of non-oil sector activity, reconstruction-related spending, and firming oil prices. As a result, the Kuwaiti financial system has returned to a strong position, with high bank profits and capitalization.

The financial sector in Kuwait is well supervised and regulated. Overall, the Central Bank has developed a supervisory process that conforms in most respects to the Core Principles for Effective Banking Supervision developed by the Basel Committee on Banking Supervision. Also, the Central Bank has adopted a comprehensive approach by establishing several procedures, including setting systemic prudential policy for financial institutions and issuing regulations and guidelines, as well as enforcing legal, regulatory, and prudential standards. In late 2001, the Central Bank drafted a law regulating money-laundering activities. Legal measures include the adoption of anti–money laundering (AML) guidelines (1997) and enactment of a law criminalizing money-laundering activities (March 2002) in accordance with the Financial Action Task Force (FATF) recommendations. The capital market was also strengthened in recent years. The government's decision to open the market to foreign investors, and to strengthen regulations regarding disclosure and insider trading, together with the general improvement in business climate, contributed to a recovery in the stock market in the past few years.

Population dynamics has led to high rate of growth of the Kuwaiti labor force in excess of 4 percent a year for much of the last decade. Nevertheless, the domestic labor market has continued to be highly dependent on expatriate workers, and has remained segmented. Most Kuwaiti workers are employed in the public sector, and most expatriate workers in the private sector. Although unemployment among Kuwaiti nationals remains low (estimated at about 2 percent), unemployment pressures are increasing, owing to the expanding Kuwaiti labor force and the unsustainable level of government hiring in the civil service, as well as the growing mismatch of skills among Kuwaiti job applicants and the requirements of the private sector. The labor market reform, approved by the National Assembly in May 2000, aimed at promoting the private sector as the main provider of jobs; making the Kuwaiti workers more attractive to private sector employers through training; limiting the allowance to public employees; and extending the social allowance to Kuwaitis in the private sector. The Manpower and Government Restructuring Program was established in July 2001 to implement the Labor Law, provide unemployment benefits and training to Kuwaiti nationals, and facilitate employment of Kuwaiti nationals in the private sector. In September 2002, the government approved quotas for the proportion of Kuwaitis that private companies must employ; companies that fail to meet this target would be subject to a fine and sanctions, such as exclusion from bidding for government contracts.

In contrast to other GCC countries, Kuwait has only recently adopted a strategy to diversify the productive base of the economy, promote the role of the private sector, and reduce government ownership and its dominance in the economy. The authorities introduced a package of reforms in 2000–01 that seeks to restore growth in the non-oil private sector (Appendix III). The economic reforms encompass a wide range of structural reforms, from the pricing of utilities and privatization to labor market reform and foreign participation in the economy. The National Assembly has passed laws on foreign portfolio investment, foreign direct investment, and key components of the labor market reform. Other major important initiatives, such as privatization law, the reform of the corporate income tax law, and the company law, are under consideration.

Oman

Continued high dependence on oil, limited oil resources, and, in particular, a rapidly rising young domestic labor force have led the Omani authorities to adopt an ambitious diversification strategy since the mid-1990s. This strategy aims at strengthening the export base centered on the development of the country's natural gas resources and promoting other non-oil activities, such as entrepôt activities and tourism.[12] In partnership with the private sector, two major achievements of this strategy were the inauguration in late 1998 of the Salalah con-

---

[11]The DCP is a debt workout scheme introduced by the government to recapitalize commercial banks that suffered losses as a result of the collapse of Souk Al-Manakh in 1982 and the Iraqi invasion. It has a favorable impact on a bank's financial situation by removing delinquent debt from its balance sheet and replacing it with government debt.

[12]Based on current proven reserves and production levels, gas resources are projected to last for some 45 years, more than double the projection for crude oil resources.

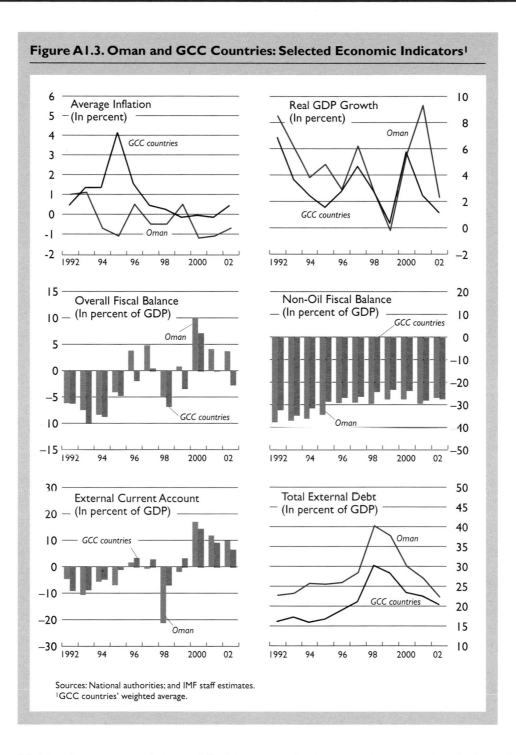

Figure A1.3. Oman and GCC Countries: Selected Economic Indicators[1]

Sources: National authorities; and IMF staff estimates.
[1]GCC countries' weighted average.

tainer port, which has become one of the world's 20 busiest and most efficient port of its kind, and the completion in 2000 of the liquefied natural gas (LNG) plant with an initial capacity of 6.6 million tons. In addition, the authorities have also built the required infrastructure—two gas pipeline networks and port —to support the development of large gas-based, outward-oriented industrial projects, such as

an aluminum smelter, petrochemicals, and fertilizer plant. Although the LNG project has contributed to an increase in Oman's external debt, the latter has remained within a manageable level (Figure A1.3).[13]

---

[13]The LNG plant has created about 350 direct jobs.

This development strategy helped sustain a relatively high real GDP growth in the hydrocarbon sector of over 4 percent a year during the last decade. However, nonhydrocarbon growth decelerated from close to 7 percent a year in the first half of the 1990s—spurred by growth in services, particularly trade—to about half that rate in the second half. Per capita GDP only increased slightly in the past decade, owing to rapid population growth. Meanwhile, as a result of declining import prices and a relatively low domestic inflation (about 0.2 percent a year on average from 1991 to 2002), the average real effective exchange rate has depreciated slightly during those years (see Table A1.1).[14]

The Omani authorities have supported their development strategy by maintaining a prudent fiscal policy. In fact, during the second half of the 1990s, government spending remained virtually unchanged in absolute terms, while non-oil revenue grew on average by 6 percent a year as a result of increases in fees and charges and improvement in revenue collection. Consequently, the overall fiscal balance (including transfers of oil revenue to the State General Reserve Fund and investment income) moved from deficits of about 7 percent of GDP in the first half of the 1990s—mostly financed by a combination of a drawdown of government foreign assets and recourse to domestic and external debt—to surpluses in the second half, except in 1998 when world oil prices collapsed.[15] The recovery in global oil prices of the past few years contributed to a turnaround in the fiscal balance, reaching surpluses of about 6 percent of GDP on average in the period 1999–2002 despite larger-than-budgeted expenditures, particularly in the area of defense. The authorities have used these surpluses to repay government debt and to build up official foreign assets. However, the increase in spending—though after almost a decade of no growth—has hindered an improvement in the non-oil/LNG fiscal deficit, which reached an estimated 25 percent of GDP in 2002.[16]

The external current account balance mirrored the fiscal performance in the past decade. From average deficits of close to 2 percent of GDP a year in the first half of the 1990s, the deficit surged to 21 percent of GDP in 1998 on account of lower oil prices

and higher LNG-related imports, before turning into surpluses in 1999–2002, reflecting the recovery in oil prices and the coming on stream of LNG exports. Also, non-oil exports (including re-exports) more than doubled in the 1990s, reaching $2.4 billion in 2002, or 22 percent of total exports.[17]

The Omani banking system consists of 15 institutions, but it is dominated by three local banks that accounted for over 70 percent of total assets at the end of 2002. All commercial banks are majority-privately owned. There are three specialized banks, two of them publicly owned, that provide long-term soft loans (subsidized by the government) for housing and small and medium-size projects. The financial system has been also strengthened in the past few years.

The Central Bank's self-assessment of its supervisory system and practices indicated that the banking system was sound, well supervised and regulated, and in compliance with the Basel Core Principles. The capital adequacy ratio exceeded the Basel Committee recommended minimum. However, the ratio of nonperforming loans to total loans has increased since 1999, reaching 11.3 percent by the end of 2000. Although the Central Bank mainly relies on indirect instruments of liquidity management, such as repo facilities and central bank certificates of deposit, a few direct controls are still in place, including quantitative ceilings on consumer loans and caps on loan interest rates—set at 40 percent of total bank lending and 11 percent a year, respectively. An anti–money laundering law was adopted in late March 2002, and Oman has taken important steps toward full compliance with FATF recommendations regarding combating terrorism financing.

The capital market is dominated by trading in government securities (development bonds and treasury bills) that are sold to both residents and nonresidents. The outstanding stock of government bonds and treasury bills stood at less than 6 percent of GDP at the end of 2001, of which local commercial banks held almost 66 percent, but secondary trading in bonds remains minimal.[18] The transparency of stock market operations improved following the adoption of the Capital Market Law in 1999. This law provides for the separation of trade, regulatory, and depositary functions of the Muscat Stock Market (MSM) and requires more stringent disclosure and reporting requirements for listed companies. These

---

[14]Oman's currency has been officially pegged to the U.S. dollar since the 1970s.

[15]Oman's prudent use of its oil revenue has contributed to the accumulation of financial wealth administered by the State General Reserve Fund—a government savings fund established in 1980 to replace dwindling oil resources. For further details see Fasano (2001a).

[16]Although dividends from the LNG project have already started to accrue to the budget, a 10-year tax holiday has been granted to the project.

[17]The Oman Center for Investment Promotion and Export Development was established in 1998 to provide the institutional support to promote non-oil activities and exports.

[18]Banks are allowed to buy a maximum of 30 percent of their net worth in development bonds, but there are no limits on the amount of treasury bills that they can hold.

reforms have, in part, boosted confidence, with the MSM rising by 26 percent in 2002 after several years of sharp losses.

Although the economy has continued to generate more jobs than can be filled by Omani nationals, unemployment pressures among Omanis have started to rise. As is the case in other GCC countries, the authorities are relying on a mix of market-based (such as improved education and vocational training) and mandatory mechanisms (such as quotas) to create job opportunities for nationals in the private sector. Moreover, large public resources have been allocated for human capital development over the medium term (close to $500 million), and private universities and colleges have been allowed to start operations in the country. At the same time, the government has provided clear signs that it will no longer be the first source of employment for nationals. On other issues, the authorities have improved Oman's national statistics significantly, with further efforts needed to collect comprehensive data on capital flows, external debt, and labor statistics.

The authorities have also stepped up structural reforms to promote growth and employment. Following a number of divestitures in banking, insurance, and tourism in the mid-1990s, the authorities have recently focused on privatizing the management of public enterprises (e.g., Salalah container port and airports) and allowing private investment in areas of services—previously the sole domain of the government. In this context, the power generation and telecommunications sectors are currently at the forefront of the privatization efforts. The installed generating capacity is being expanded through independent power projects under a build-own-operate basis. Following the regional trend, the authorities recently lifted impediments to foreign direct investment, significantly reduced the corporate income tax bias against foreign companies, and streamlined regulations to improve the business climate and attract foreign investment. Moreover, ahead of other countries in the GCC area, the Omani government has already reduced industrial incentives, including limiting the maximum amount of soft loans and bringing the cost of these loans closer to market interest rates to enhance the role of market mechanisms to improve resource allocation.

Qatar

Qatar experienced a dramatic turnaround in economic performance in the second half of the 1990s. Facing a need to revitalize growth—after a period of lukewarm economic growth during much of the 1980s and early 1990s—and to break away from its dependence on oil (projected to last only 15 years,

based on current production levels and proven reserves), the country turned to its large untapped reserves of natural gas to develop the LNG sector, as well as to further expand export-oriented, energy-intensive industries, such as petrochemicals, steel, and fertilizers, and recently, tourism.[19] As a result, real aggregate GDP growth surged to about 10 percent a year, on average, between 1997 and 2002, compared with 2.5 percent during 1990–96, leading to a sharp increase in per capita income. Qatar borrowed heavily in international markets to finance the development strategy. The total external debt is estimated to have reached about $16 billion or 84 percent of GDP at end-2002, though the LNG debt service is tied to proceeds from its exports.

Despite diversification efforts, the Qatari economy is still dominated by the public sector, with the oil and gas sectors—majority-owned by the government—accounting for almost half of real GDP in 2001, and government services for an estimated 17 percent. The government also owns substantial equity in a number of business entities, including the largest bank in the country (Qatar National Bank). Partially reflecting the dominance of the government in the economy, nonhydrocarbon growth has remained subdued, averaging close to 3 percent a year through 1996 and less than 2 percent since 1998—though it is estimated that it has accelerated to 4 percent in 2002, owing to industrial projects under way. Meanwhile, the pegged exchange rate regime has contributed to keeping Qatar's inflation low (about 2.5 percent a year on average from 1991 to 2002 though in 1996, the CPI increased by about 7 percent owing to the adjustment in some fees and charges). However, inflation has been higher than the GCC average and its main trading partners, contributing to an appreciation of the real effective exchange rate of close to 20 percent during the past decade.

Qatar's financial position has improved dramatically since 1999. The rise in LNG production—combined with the boost in crude oil output and the strong recovery in global oil prices of the past few years—has turned the country's external current account balance into a surplus of more than 10 percent of GDP since 1999 (after it averaged deficits of close to 19 percent of GDP during much of the 1990s, owing in part to the surge in LNG-related imports). At the same time, Qatar moved vigorously to hold the line on public expenditures, which grew by 18 percent from 1996/97 to 2001/02 (the fiscal year is from April to March), even though oil revenues almost doubled over the same period (Figure A1.4).

---

[19]Qatar has become the largest Middle East producer of chemical fertilizers and some petrochemical products, and the fourth largest LNG exporter in the world.

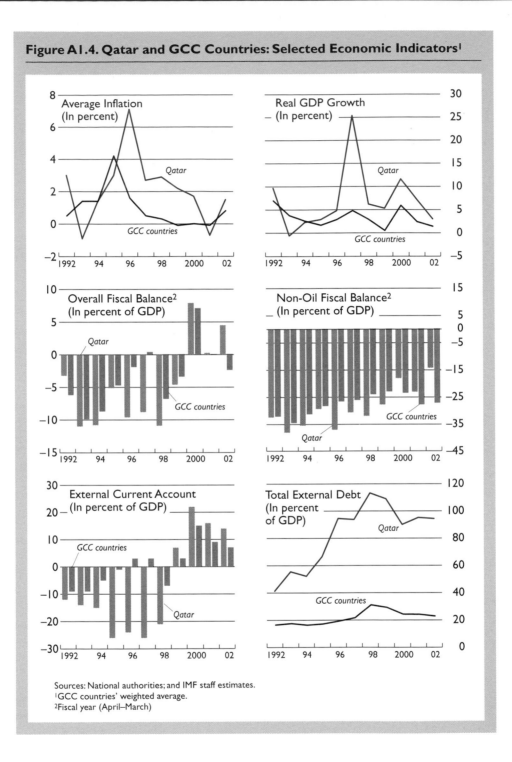

Figure A1.4. Qatar and GCC Countries: Selected Economic Indicators[1]

Average Inflation (In percent)

Real GDP Growth (In percent)

Overall Fiscal Balance[2] (In percent of GDP)

Non-Oil Fiscal Balance[2] (In percent of GDP)

External Current Account (In percent of GDP)

Total External Debt (In percent of GDP)

Sources: National authorities; and IMF staff estimates.
[1]GCC countries' weighted average.
[2]Fiscal year (April–March)

Fiscal retrenchment has taken the form of reform of the electricity and water sector, layoffs of expatriate government workers, and the restructuring of ministries. Consequently, the overall fiscal balance (including investment income) switched from deficits of over 6 percent of GDP on average during much of the 1990s to a surplus of about 4 percent of GDP, on average, in the past few years, with much of the recent windfall oil gains going toward building up government foreign assets. Largely because of the restrained expenditure, the non-oil/LNG fiscal deficit in relation to GDP has improved significantly since 1999/2000, reaching an estimated 15 percent of GDP in 2002/03.

Notwithstanding the conservative fiscal stance, the structure of the budget remains vulnerable to oil price shocks—albeit less than in the past. On average, the budget received 66 percent of total revenue from oil sales in the 1990s, followed by government investment income, which accounted for 25 percent of the total during the same period. Non-oil revenue (excluding investment income) has remained low, ranging between 3–4 percent of GDP during much of the past decade, as the government has been reluctant to adopt a modern and broad-based tax system. On the expenditure side, the welfare system and industrial incentives remain highly generous, including government services provided free or at highly subsidized rates, despite high per capita income and living standards.

The financial and capital sectors have been strengthened in the past few years. In 1997, the Doha Securities Market (DSM) was created, increasing on average by 16 percent a year through the end of 2001. However, the DSM still remains closed to foreign investors. The Central Bank has raised the minimum capital adequacy ratio to 10 percent and completed the liberalization of interest rates on deposits in local currency, though a recently created public development bank provides long-term soft loans. Moreover, the reserve requirements were simplified by setting unremunerated cash reserves equal to 2.75 percent of total deposits (including foreign deposits) instead of 19 percent of total demand deposits previously in effect. The Central Bank has also introduced a new short-term instrument, the Qatar monetary rate (QMR) effective April 1, 2002, to enhance liquidity management. The interest rate associated with this facility serves as a benchmark for the money market. Commercial banks can now deposit their excess liquidity in this facility and earn interest at the QMR, instead of sending it abroad, as was previously the case. The Central Bank also tightened nonperforming loan classification criteria and required banks to appoint independent auditors to assess provisioning levels.

Qatar's financial sector is well capitalized and supervised and remains quite profitable. However, although there are 15 banks in the country, the Qatar National Bank—50 percent owned by the government—accounted for a large portion of the sector's total assets (over 50 percent) at the end of 2000. Also, banks hold most of the government's domestic debt in the form of treasury bills and bonds. Monetary policy continues to be constrained by the pegged exchange rate regime and currency board–type arrangement in place that requires maintaining 100 percent foreign exchange coverage of local currency issues. For liquidity management, the Central Bank mostly relies on unremunerated reserve requirements, loans-to-deposit ratio, and trading of treasury bills and bonds. A new banking law, designed to strengthen the independence of the Central Bank and enhance its supervision role,

is awaiting approval. In line with the FATF guidelines, the authorities have also completed a draft anti–money laundering law, which is presently undergoing the process of approval.

The development strategy benefited greatly from a series of broad structural reforms aimed at increasing the role of the private sector by partially privatizing public enterprises and/or management, as well as creating a business-friendly regulatory environment. The first major sale of public assets took place at the end of 1998, when the government sold 45 percent of its share in the telecommunications company in the local stock market for about $650 million, but since then the privatization program has stalled. Major progress has been made in restructuring the power sector. The first independent power and water plant is presently under construction, and will be operated on a build-own-operate basis. The government has also taken several measures in recent years to promote investment, including revising the company and agency laws to foster domestic competition and allowing foreign investors to own 100 percent of companies in agriculture, industry, health, education, and tourism. A one-stop window was also established in 2002 for prospective domestic and foreign investors in order to expedite the process of license and land approval. Other developments under way include the partial privatization of a government company that distributes gasoline locally, and the corporatization of postal and aviation services. A new agency law under consideration seeks to reduce the monopoly power of sole agents by allowing anybody to import any good on a commercial basis subject to paying a negotiable fee of up to 5 percent of the imported value to the existing agent.

Unemployment among Qatari nationals is currently thought to be low (no official data are available), as the number of graduates from secondary and tertiary educational institutions is small. Nevertheless, demographic dynamics point toward a rapidly growing indigenous labor force over the medium term, since about one-fourth of the population is at present under the age of 15. Thus, Qatar's labor policy centers on efforts to gradually increase the proportion of Qataris in the labor force, particularly in the private sector, through market-based mechanisms, including appropriate training and education. By contrast, limited progress has been achieved so far in improving the quality of the country's national statistics and public access to updated economic and financial data.

Overall, Qatar's development strategy has increased its ability to weather adverse oil shocks. Long-term contracts with Asian, Indian, and European firms mean the volume of LNG exports is likely to surge to over 20 million tons by 2005, toppling crude oil as the most important Qatari export

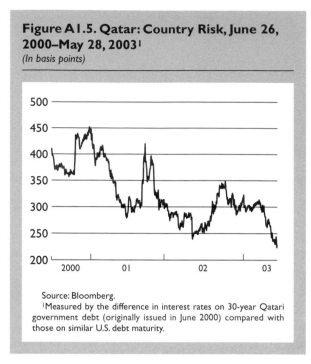

Figure A1.5. Qatar: Country Risk, June 26, 2000–May 28, 2003[1]

(In basis points)

Source: Bloomberg.
[1]Measured by the difference in interest rates on 30-year Qatari government debt (originally issued in June 2000) compared with those on similar U.S. debt maturity.

(see Fasano 2001b).[20] These strong fundamentals have been reflected in declining country risk in the past year as perceived by the international capital markets (Figure A1.5).

Saudi Arabia

Saudi Arabia's economic performance has improved in recent years, after having recorded relatively low economic growth during much of the 1990s. As a result of this weak performance and a rapidly increasing young labor force, strains in the employment market for Saudi nationals have emerged, and income per head has stagnated. However, in the past few years, the authorities have strengthened the process of structural reforms and intensified the diversification drive. Consequently, while real non-oil GDP growth averaged 1.8 percent a year from 1991 to 1999, it accelerated to close to 4 percent in the following three years. In contrast, cuts in oil output in 2001–02 to stabilize global crude oil prices have caused total real GDP growth to slow to about 1 percent a year (Figure A1.6). Private sector activity, which accounts for almost 60 percent of the non-oil sector, has become less depen-

dent on the stimulus of government spending.[21] This is evident by the continued growth of private investment despite restrained expenditure growth in the past years. Meanwhile, Saudi Arabia's inflation has been one of the lowest in the GCC area (about 0.5 percent on average from 1991 to 2002). As a result, the real effective exchange rate has depreciated slightly, even though the U.S. dollar, to which the local currency is pegged, has strengthened in international markets until recently (see Table A1.1).

Saudi Arabia's financial position improved in 2000, reflecting the strong recovery in global oil prices.[22] Indeed, after having registered on average deficits of about 7 percent of GDP during much of the 1990s, the central government's overall budgetary accounts moved to a surplus of 3.2 percent of GDP in 2000 before returning to a deficit of about 4 percent in the following year. Many years of deficits have contributed to a sharp increase in the government domestic debt, which reached 90 percent of GDP by the end of 2001, with over two-thirds being held by government agencies, such as pension funds. In 2002, the overall fiscal deficit is estimated to have risen to 6 percent of GDP, with government domestic debt ratio increasing further. The country's underlying fiscal position has also deteriorated, with a non-oil deficit estimated at about 30 percent of GDP from 23 percent in 1998–99. As in the case of other GCC countries, the budget structure remains weak, with the wage bill estimated to have reached about 17 percent of GDP in 2002— one of the highest level in the region.

After recording deficits during much of the 1990s, the external current account balance has presented a surplus since 2000. Non-oil exports (mainly petrochemicals and manufactured goods) more than doubled in the 1990s, reaching close to $9 billion in 2002—the second highest level in the GCC area after the United Arab Emirates. Despite current account deficits throughout much of the 1990s, net foreign assets of the Saudi Arabian Monetary Agency (SAMA) have remained at a comfortable position (equivalent to about nine months of imports of goods and services in 2002).

The Saudi banking system is considered to be sound. Banks enjoy high profitability, the capital adequacy ratio is over 20 percent, and nonperforming loans are low. SAMA has also assigned high priority

---

[20]The government has indicated that beginning in the coming years, the budget is likely to start receiving dividends and other revenues from LNG exports. This, coupled with declining debt and interest payments, would help maintain a strong fiscal position.

[21]See Fasano and Wang (2001) on the relationship between government spending and non-oil growth in GCC countries.

[22]Following the end of the 1991 regional conflict, Saudi Arabia has devoted increased attention to fiscal consolidation. As a result of cuts that affected most categories of expenditure, the overall fiscal deficit returned to the pre-conflict level in nominal terms by 1995. But the second half of the 1990s witnessed renewed volatility in government spending, reflecting the fluctuation in oil prices.

Figure A1.6. Saudi Arabia and GCC Countries: Selected Economic Indicators[1]

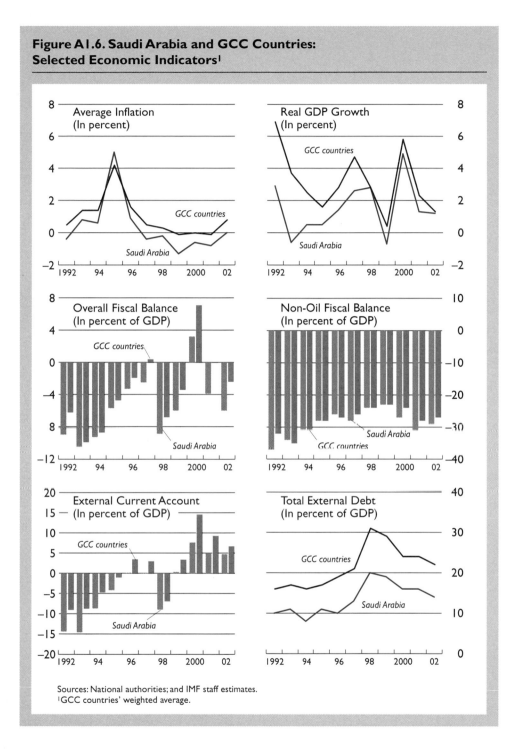

Average Inflation
(In percent)

GCC countries

Saudi Arabia

Real GDP Growth
(In percent)

GCC countries

Saudi Arabia

Overall Fiscal Balance
(In percent of GDP)

GCC countries

Saudi Arabia

Non-Oil Fiscal Balance
(In percent of GDP)

Saudi Arabia

GCC countries

External Current Account
(In percent of GDP)

GCC countries

Saudi Arabia

Total External Debt
(In percent of GDP)

GCC countries

Saudi Arabia

Sources: National authorities; and IMF staff estimates.
[1]GCC countries' weighted average.

to appropriate prudential regulations and close supervision of banks. In addition, compared with other GCC countries, the banking system is not highly concentrated, with 2 local banks out of 11 accounting for about one-fourth of total assets. Efforts to further deepen and broaden the capital market have been enhanced. The government is presently in the process of adopting a new capital markets' law that will help mobilize resources, enhance transparency, clearly define listing requirements for companies, and establish a securities and exchange commission to regulate the functioning of the stock exchange. Monetary policy continues to be constrained by the pegged exchange rate regime and the currency board–type arrangement in place, which requires maintaining 100 percent foreign exchange coverage of local currency issues. For liquidity management, the central bank mostly relies on indirect instruments of liquidity management, especially repo operations in government bonds and foreign exchange swaps with banks.

Saudi Arabia has taken a leading position on the introduction of the anti–money laundering legislation in the area. An anti–money laundering law was passed in May 1999 in line with recently mandated international guidelines.

Saudi Arabia has recently made progress in advancing broad structural reforms that aim primarily at encouraging foreign investment and enhancing the role of the private sector. Ongoing key reforms include institutional strengthening of economic policy-making, the restructuring of state enterprises and privatization, and revision of the foreign investment law—allowing foreign investors full ownership of business in most economic sectors.[23] In the area of privatization, a sequential strategy aims initially at privatizing management, and then divestment, deregulation, and finally privatization. While there is no firm timetable for privatization, the primary focus, in the short run, will be on the corporatization of enterprises, and on establishing the associated regulatory frameworks (mainly in the electricity, telecommunications, and transportation sectors) in order to prepare for their eventual privatization without creating private sector monopolies. Saudi Arabia offered 30 percent of the shares of the Saudi Telecommunications Company for sale to the private sector in December 2002. The revision of a number of laws (e.g., company, agency, competition, mortgage lending, capital markets) is under way to promote private sector activity and foster domestic competition.

To create employment opportunities for a rapidly rising global labor force, the authorities have in place a strategy that consists of skills development and correction of labor market distortions. The Human Resource Development Fund was recently established to finance the training of Saudi nationals for jobs in demand by the private sector, while a database to help match Saudis seeking employment in the private sector with job openings is being developed. As regards other reforms, Saudi Arabia's external tariffs were recently reduced to 5 percent from 12 percent in accordance with the GCC common external tariff adopted in early 2003. Efforts are also under way to complete negotiations to join the

World Trade Organization. In addition, substantial progress has been achieved in improving the quality, timeliness, and dissemination of data.

United Arab Emirates

The United Arab Emirates is a confederation of seven emirates that hold considerable political, judicial, financial, and economic autonomy.[24] Overall, the U.A.E. economy has developed within a highly liberal, business-friendly, and market-oriented economic policy framework. Real GDP rose at an average annual rate of about 5 percent during the 1990s, double the growth rate in the 1980s, as development efforts intensified, particularly in non-oil activities. As a result, the U.A.E. economy is one of the most diversified in the GCC area, with petrochemicals, aluminum, tourism, banking, and entrepôt trade activities currently accounting for a large share of GDP. Moreover, the United Arab Emirates—the sixth largest world crude oil exporter—has systematically recorded a trade- and income-driven external current account surplus, and remained a net creditor nation. The country has accumulated substantial official foreign assets, providing ample latitude to respond to oil price shocks. A pegged exchange rate—effectively fixed to the U.S. dollar—has served as a nominal anchor for the economy since the early 1980s. However, with an average annual inflation of 3.5 percent from 1991 to 2002, the REER appreciated substantially during those years—though there is no evidence so far that this appreciation has hindered the performance of non-oil exports or economic growth.

The United Arab Emirates generally recorded small consolidated fiscal deficits during the 1990s, mostly financed through changes in government foreign assets (Figure A1.7).[25] These deficits averaged about 2 percent of GDP. However, rising global oil prices in 2000 contributed to a sharp improvement in the fiscal accounts, which reached a surplus of 6 percent of GDP despite a surge in expenditure, mostly on account of higher defense and

---

[23]Preliminary data point to the positive impact of the new sponsorship and foreign investment laws on private sector investment, as the government has approved projects by foreign investors worth more than $10 billion since 2000.

[24]The seven emirates are Abu Dhabi, Dubai, Sharjah, Ajman, Umm al Qaiwain, Ras al Khaimah, and Fujairah. There are important differences among individual emirates because of the uneven distribution of oil and gas. The Emirate of Abu Dhabi is the largest one, accounting for 90 percent of the country's oil reserves and about half of total GDP, while it has the highest per capita income in the country (about five times higher than the income in the poorest emirate). Dubai—the second largest emirate—accounts for one-fourth of the country's total GDP and has been at the forefront of developing non-oil activities in anticipation of the depletion of its crude oil reserves over the medium term.

[25]Fiscal data consolidate federal and the four largest emirate governments, including investment income.

Figure A1.7. United Arab Emirates and GCC Countries: Selected Economic Indicators[1]

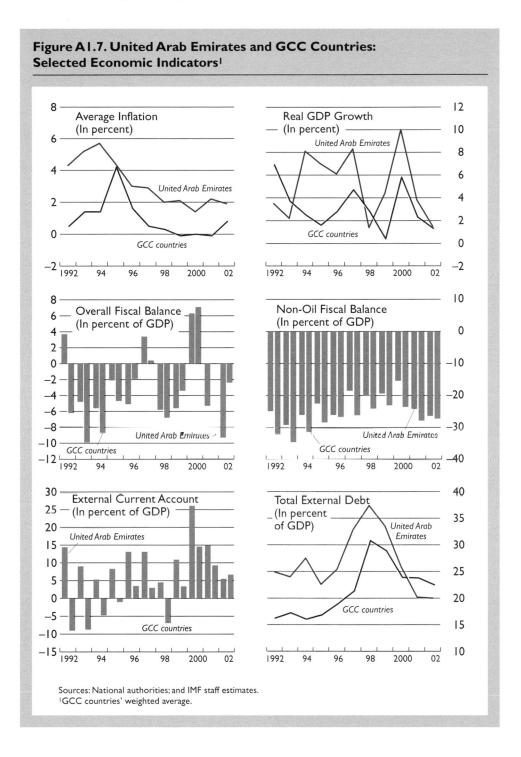

Sources: National authorities; and IMF staff estimates.
[1]GCC countries' weighted average.

subsidies. In 2001–02, the overall fiscal balance switched to a large deficit reflecting the high level of spending and lower oil revenue and investment income (owing to declining global interest rates). Mirroring these developments, the non-oil fiscal deficit widened significantly, reaching an estimated 26 percent of GDP or about Dh 68 billion in 2002—

almost double the level registered in the mid-1990s. In addition, the rapid expansion of non-oil activities has not generated a corresponding increase in non-oil revenue due to the absence of a developed tax system, with oil revenue as a share of total government revenue remaining high (in the range of 40–60 percent in recent years).

As is the case in other GCC countries, an open economy, liberal capital flows, and the exchange rate peg entail limited scope for an independent monetary policy in the United Arab Emirates. As a result, domestic interest rates have closely tracked movements in U.S. rates. In this context, the main monetary policy instruments of the Central Bank are reserve requirements for the commercial banks, and, since the government does not issue securities, its own certificates of deposit (CD).

Banks in the United Arab Emirates are broadly profitable and well supervised. Net profits of the banking system—consisting of 46 banks, 20 locally incorporated and 26 branches of foreign banks—have averaged about 12 percent since 1996. In 2001, a World Bank–IMF Financial Sector Assessment Program (FSAP) was carried out in the United Arab Emirates. The assessment generally endorsed the soundness and strong supervision of the banking sector, although oversight of insurance companies was felt to be in need of improvement.[26] Since the end of 2000, the Central Bank has stepped up efforts to combat money laundering and terrorism financing. A new anti–money laundering law came into effect in early 2002 while the supervision of the "hawala" system of informal money transfers has been strengthened.

With energy demands surging in the United Arab Emirates, power generation and water desalination are at the forefront of privatization efforts. In particular, Abu Dhabi has embarked on new power projects through joint ventures with foreign investors, and selling of some existing assets. Other structural reforms under way at the federal level are a comprehensive reform of public expenditure management and other fiscal initiatives, including the adoption of an electronic government project. A number of steps, such as the enactment of the Federal Securities Law and the creation of the Emirates Securities and Commodities Markets Authority, have been adopted to address deficiencies in the capital market, with formal stock exchanges (in Abu Dhabi and Dubai) opening in 2000. Meanwhile, restrictions on foreign ownership of companies and properties remain in place, including a maximum 49 percent foreign ownership of companies. But these restrictions have had little practical effect because, other than Abu Dhabi, the emirates have established free zones that allow 100 percent foreign ownership of companies. Moreover, Dubai has recently allowed foreigners to own land and properties in some real estate development, contributing to a construction boom. It also announced in 2002 the launch of several new free zones that aim to establish the emirate as a global hub for trade in gold bullion, research and development of technology, and financial activities.

Given the relatively small indigenous population and an open-border foreign labor policy, the labor market is heavily dependent on expatriate workers. Although there is currently no evidence of unemployment among U.A.E. nationals, strains are likely to appear in the period ahead as a result of population dynamics. The authorities are focusing on improving education and intensifying training to enhance the employability of nationals, particularly in the private sector, while avoiding the widespread use of mandatory measures to hire nationals, such as quotas.[27] The National Human Resource Development and Employment Authority was created in 2001 to help improve the skills of nationals looking for jobs, and a national labor database is being established to facilitate employment search efforts.

---

[26]The Financial Sector Stability Assessment report (IMF, 2003) is available on the IMF's external website (http://www.imf.org/external/pubs/cat/).

[27]Quotas are currently only applied in the banking sector.

Appendix II. GCC Countries: Comparative Tax Rates and Incentives

	Bahrain	Kuwait	Oman	Qatar	Saudi Arabia	United Arab Emirates
Tax rates						
On individuals						
Nationals	None.	None.	None.	None.	None.	None.
Foreigners (self-employed)	None.	None.	None.	None.	Progressive tax structure, with rates ranging from 5 percent (on income of SRls 16,000) to 30 percent (on income over SRls 66,000), with a tax-free threshold of SRls 6,000.	None.
On corporate income						
Local companies	None.	None.	0 percent for taxable income up to RO 30,000, and 12 percent for income above RO 30,000.	None.	None.	None.
Oil companies	46 percent.	55 percent and special arrangements.	55 percent.	85 percent.	85 percent.	55 percent (Abu Dhabi); 50 percent (Dubai).
Foreign companies	None, except foreign banks, which are subject to a fee.	Progressive tax structure with rates ranging from 5 percent (for income between KD 5,250–18,750) to 55 percent (above KD 375,000).	Companies with up to 70 percent foreign ownership are taxed as domestic companies; companies with more than 70 percent foreign ownership are subject to a progressive tax structure with rates ranging from 0 percent to 30 percent.	Progressive tax structure with rates ranging from 0 percent for profits up to QR 0.1 million to 35 percent for over QR 5 million. However, the maximum rate was recently reduced to 30 percent.	Progressive tax structure with rates ranging from 15 percent (on first SRls 100,000) to 30 percent (on over SRls 100,000).	Only foreign banks are taxed at 20 percent on profits.
Customs duties	Single 5 percent on most products; 0 percent for foodstuffs; and 100 percent on tobacco and alcoholic beverages.	Single 5 percent on most products; 0 percent for foodstuffs; and 100 percent on tobacco and alcoholic beverages.	Single 5 percent on most products; 0 percent for foodstuffs; and 100 percent on tobacco and alcoholic beverages.	Single 5 percent on most products; 0 percent for foodstuffs; and 100 percent on tobacco and alcoholic beverages.	Single 5 percent on most products; 0 percent for foodstuffs; and 100 percent on tobacco and alcoholic beverages.	Single 5 percent on most products; 0 percent for foodstuffs; and 100 percent on tobacco and alcoholic beverages.
Export duties	None.	4 percent on all goods not subject to import duties.	None.	None.	None.	None.

Appendix II (concluded)

	Bahrain	Kuwait	Oman	Qatar	Saudi Arabia	United Arab Emirates
Social security contributions	Employer 10 percent, employee 5 percent.	Employer 10 percent, employee 5 percent.	Employer 9 percent, employee 5 percent, and government 2 percent (private sector).	None currently, but under consideration.	Employer 8 percent, employee 5 percent.	Employer 12.5 percent, employee 5 percent, and government 2.5 percent (private sector).
Other taxes	Municipal taxes: 10 percent of rent on commercial property. Training levy: companies with more than 50 employees have to provide training schemes or pay training levy of 2 percent of Bahraini wage bill or 4 percent of foreign usage bill.	Property transfer tax is 0.5 percent of value. Kuwaiti shareholding companies are required to donate to research and development of 5 percent net profit to Kuwait Foundation for the Advancement of Sciences.	Training tax: applicable to all companies with more than 20 employees. The rate is a flat RO 100 annually. Companies providing specified training for their Omani employees are exempt from the training tax. Municipal taxes: 2 percent on electricity, 3 percent on tenancy contracts and airline tickets, 5 percent on hotels and restaurants, and 10 percent on cinemas and amusement parks.			Municipal taxes vary among emirates: 5 percent rental taxes and 5 percent hotel taxes in Dubai and Abu Dhabi.
Tax and other incentives	Cost of exploratory well can be deducted at 20 percent. Direct subsidies for electricity and provision of water and sewerage services at below economic cost.	Tax holidays: up to 10 years. Exemption from customs duty on imports of capital equipment and raw materials.	Tax holidays: 5 years and renewable for a period not exceeding 5 years. Customs duty exemptions.	Tax holidays: up to 10 years, depending on the nature of the investment and business, and utilities services are subsidized. Also, imports of raw materials not available in Qatar are duty free. Operating losses can be carried forward for up to 3 years.	No tax holidays to Saudi nationals or foreigners on new investments under the revised foreign investment law enacted in April 2000. Incentives are allowed to run their course on existing investments; these included 10-year tax holidays on agricultural and manufacturing projects, and a 5-year tax holiday for other economic projects. Exemptions from customs duties for imports of machinery and raw materials, nominal rents for plant, industrial building, and workers' living quarters.	Tax holidays: 15 years, renewable in most free zones.

Sources: National authorities; and PriceWaterhouseCoopers, *Corporate Taxes: Worldwide Summaries 1999–2000.*

Appendix III. GCC Countries: Summary of Recent Key Structural Reforms in Selected Areas

	Bahrain	Kuwait	Oman	Qatar	Saudi Arabia	United Arab Emirates
Administrative reforms	Approval of the Early Retirement Scheme in April 2000 to facilitate downsizing labor in some government agencies. Adoption of a Public Expenditure Management Strategy initiative to increase cost recovery on government services, contracting out publicly provided services, and corporatization and eventual privatization of selected government activities. Review of the government's expenditure management system to establish a medium- to long-term framework for more efficient budgetary planning while reaching a balanced budget by 2006 (under way).	Appointment of a new Higher Committee for Development and Economic Reform (2001) to facilitate the reform process.	Amending the commercial company law to eliminate the sole agency monopoly. Restructuring the Public Telecommunications Authority into a closed company, and liquidating the Public Authority for Agriculture. Establishing a one-stop service for prospective local and foreign investors.	The ministries of electricity and water and of telecommunications and transport were abolished and their functions were transferred to autonomous public-private partnerships operating on a commercial basis. The ministry of telecommunications and transport was broken up into three autonomous corporations.	Establishment of the Supreme Economic Council to oversee and coordinate economic policy (August 1999). Establishment of the Supreme Council for Petroleum and Mineral Affairs to formulate policies on hydrocarbons and supervision of ARAMCO (January 2000). Establishment of the Higher Tourism Authority to encourage international tourism (November 2000).	Adoption of "e-Government" initiative in Dubai; and similar initiatives at the federal level.

Appendix III (continued)

	Bahrain	Kuwait	Oman	Qatar	Saudi Arabia	United Arab Emirates
Financial sector reform	Ratifying anti–money laundering legislation. Enforcing Bahrain Stock Exchange rules and regulations and suspending non-compliant companies. Issuing the first Islamic government bills to complement the working of the Islamic financial institutions, and taking steps toward improving prudential regulations for Islamic banking. Establishing an Islamic rating agency and Islamic Securities Market (under way).	Portfolio foreign investment law (approved September 2000). Under this law, foreigners are allowed to own and trade shares of joint-stock companies listed on the Kuwait Stock Exchange, subject to specific limits.	Expanding repo facilities to the interbank market. Adoption of a capital market law to restructure the Muscat Securities Market into three separate bodies dealing with regulations, trading and exchange, and depository registration. Adoption of a new banking law in 2000. Tightening central bank supervision to reduce the risk of overlending to individuals, corporations, and related parties; strengthening risk management.	Removal of deposit interest ceilings in 2000; closer bank supervision, resulting in tightening of nonperforming loan criteria. A new short-term instrument has been introduced by the Central Bank to enhance liquidity management. Under the scheme, commercial banks can deposit their excess liquidity with the Central Bank and receive interest at the newly established Qatar monetary rate.	Allowing foreigners to trade on the stock market through open-ended mutual funds. Approval of new capital markets law by the Shoura to deepen the financial markets and strengthen the stock market (January 2003).	Strengthened Central Bank supervision in 1998–99; in 2000, formal stock markets and regulatory body for capital markets were established; provisions for anti-money laundering were completed with the 2000 law, and along with provisions for combating the financing of terrorism became federal law in January 2002; a third Islamic bank (National Bank of Sharjah) became operational; new Securities Law was enacted in 2000 to address volatility and malpractices that plagued the securities market in 1997 and 1998; a comprehensive pilot risk-management module for banks is being implemented; a new insurance law is being drafted to bring the local market in line with international standards.
Foreign investment	Easing rules on non-GCC firms to own buildings and lease land, and establishing a one-stop shop to facilitate licensing procedures. Ratifying the amendment to the GCC	Foreign Direct Investment (FDI) Law (passed April 2001) to allow foreigners to own 100 percent of Kuwaiti companies. Under the new law, corporate taxes were	Reduction of income tax disparity between Omani and foreign companies by raising the single rate for the former to 12 percent from 7.5 percent, and lowering the rates for the latter to 5–30	In 2000, the Company, Foreign Investment, and Agency Laws were simplified, including allowing 100 percent foreign ownership in agriculture, industry, health, education, and tourism sectors, and	Enactment of a new Investment Law and establishment of the associated investment authority (SAGIA) to facilitate foreign direct investment processing, including the establishment of one-	Foreign ownership remains limited to no more than 49 percent by federal law, except in free zones, where 100 percent is possible. Dubai announced the launch of several new

free zones intended to establish the emirate as a global center for trade in gold bullion, research and development of technology, and financial activities.

stop shop (April 2000). Permission for 100 percent foreign ownership of business, except for about 22 activities, subject to annual revision. In February 2001, gas, power generation, water desalination, and petrochemicals were removed from the negative list. Cut the highest corporate income tax on foreign investment from 45 percent to 30 percent (May 2000).

streamlining investment approval procedures.

The maximum corporate tax has been reduced from 35 percent to 30 percent.

percent from 15–50 percent.

Redefining "foreign" company as one with more than 70 percent foreign ownership instead of 49 percent.

Allowing foreign, non-GCC firms to own buildings and lease land.

Opening up the service sector to full foreign ownership in line with WTO agreements.

reduced to 25 percent from 55 percent. Companies would enjoy a tax holiday of 10 years, exemptions from customs duty on imports of capital equipment and raw materials, and permission to bring in necessary foreign labor.

A Foreign Investment Capital Office was established to process foreign direct investment applications.

Common Economic Agreement, by which the national origin of a traded good became solely defined in terms of the source of its value added.

Foreign ownership permitted to increase from 49 percent to 100 percent of businesses in all but a few strategic sectors (e.g., oil and aluminum).

Establishment of one-stop shop to facilitate foreign investment licensing procedures.

Reduction of external tariff to 5 percent from 5.5 percent and 7 percent.

State enterprise reform and privatization	Privatized the public slaughter house and the capital's waste collection and incineration. Other privatizations are under way, including the public transport company (bus) and tourism facilities. The telecommunications and postal services sectors are being liberalized.	The privatization law, approved by the Finance Committee of the National Assembly, establishes a comprehensive framework for large-scale privatization, identifies areas and modes of privatization, and sets up a pricing mechanism and safeguards against job losses. The government plans to offer for sale to the private sector most of the 62 public sector entities still under its control.	The power sector is at the forefront of privatization efforts, with three power plants now under construction by foreign investors under a build-own-operate basis. Existing government power plants are being restructured for their future privatization. Oman has also recently privatized the management of airport services. Other services to be privatized in the near future include water distribution, waste water network, postal services, and telecommunications. The government also plans to gradually sell its participation in the few remaining non-oil public companies listed in the local stock market.	Partially privatized the Telecommunications Company at end-1998. Corporatized the electricity and water sector and sold most of the government's power generation plants to Qatar Electricity and Water Company, which is majority-owned by the local private sector. Construction is under way of the first independent power and water plant, which is majority-owned by a foreign developer. Sold 60 percent of the government's stake in a recently created company—spun off from Qatar Petroleum—to take over the local distribution of gasoline.	Announced in June 2002 a new privatization strategy under which management would be given autonomy, followed by deregulation (corporatization) and ultimately private ownership. Twenty sectors are presently identified for privatization, including telecommunications, electricity, industrial parks, postal services, water, railroad, education, and air transportation. Saudi Arabia has recently privatized 30 percent of the Saudi Telecommunications Company. Eight regional electricity companies have been merged into the Saudi Electricity Company, and a regulatory authority was established to set tariff rates and regulate market access to new entrants.	Introduced utility privatization, embarking on new power projects through joint ventures with foreign investors, and selling some existing assets.

Appendix III (concluded)

	Bahrain	Kuwait	Oman	Qatar	Saudi Arabia	United Arab Emirates
Real estate	Except for GCC nationals, the purchase of real estate by non-GCC nationals is generally prohibited, but there are exceptions.	GCC nationals may purchase real estate for private residence purposes.	No controls.	GCC nationals may purchase real estate for private residence purposes.	Permitting non-Saudis to own real estate for their business or residence, except in the two holy cities (May 2001).	The Emirate of Dubai recently relaxed restrictions on foreign investment in specific real estate projects.
Labor market reform	Developing a new two-year National Employment Strategy in cooperation with the International Labor Organization, this includes providing fiscal subsidies for training nationals in the private sector, and financial aid for the unemployed. Introducing new measures to improve general education standards, and vocational and technical training programs. Abolishing "free visa" system to expatriate labor force. Implementation of order to increase employment quota of Bahrainis in small and medium-size companies; lowering quotas for construction sector from 50 percent of Bahrainis on payroll to 15 percent (under way).	The labor market law (for National Labor Support and Encouragement to Work in Non-Government Sectors) was approved by the National Assembly on May 10, 2000, and is designed to encourage Kuwaitis to seek employment in the private sector. The Manpower and Government Restructuring Program (MGRP) was established in July 2001 to implement the labor law, provide unemployment benefits to unemployed Kuwaiti nationals, and provide training and facilitate employment of Kuwaiti nationals in the private sector. In September 2002, the government approved quotas for the proportion of Kuwaitis that private companies must employ; companies that fail to meet this target would be subject to a fine and sanctions such as exclusion from bidding for government contracts.	Introducing measures to improve vocational and technical training programs, and passing new legislation that allows private universities and colleges. Modernizing the educational system at all levels. Setting a uniform minimum wage for Omanis at RO 100 (plus RO 20 as transportation allowance) instead of the previous two-tiered (skilled/unskilled) minimum wage. New ministry of manpower created in 2002. New labor law approved in May 2003.	The government has formally ended the policy of automatic employment for graduates. It now assists jobseekers by maintaining information on job openings and by counseling and training. A department has been established in the Ministry of Civil Service with responsibility for this function.	Creation of the Human Resources Development Fund (HRDF)—with financial participation of the private sector—to provide training of Saudi labor force in skills required by the private sector, and development of a database for matching and placement of Saudi workers in the private sector (November 2000).	The National Human Resource Development and Employment Authority were created in 2001 to help improve skills of U.A.E nationals looking for jobs; a national labor market database is being established to facilitate job search.

Source: IMF staff based on information provided by the national authorities.

Appendix IV Experience of Selected Monetary Unions

There are currently five monetary unions—three in Africa, one in the Caribbean, and one in Europe.[1] Two unions in Africa are part of the CFA franc zone and comprise the West African Economic and Monetary Union (WAEMU), which has eight members, and the Central African Economic and Monetary Community (CAEMC), which has six members.[2] Each regional grouping issues its own CFA franc, but they are exchangeable one-for-one against each other and are pegged to the euro. The Common Monetary Area (CMA) includes four members in southern Africa (Lesotho, Namibia, South Africa, and Swaziland). The South African currency, the rand, is the common currency in operation in this union, although the other countries have retained their own currencies, which are pegged to the rand, and their central banks function as currency boards.

The fourth currency area, the Eastern Caribbean Currency Union (ECCU), is constituted by eight small island economies that share a single currency, the Eastern Caribbean dollar, and a central bank. The Eastern Caribbean dollar was pegged to the British pound from 1950 to 1976, and since then, it has been pegged to the U.S. dollar. The fifth monetary union currently in existence—the European Economic and Monetary Union (EMU)—is the most recent and by far the most economically important (see Table 3.1). Although the euro has been in existence only since January 1, 1999, the EMU's extensive process of institutional preparation for a common central bank and a new currency, as well as the efforts invested in macroeconomic convergence, provide important lessons for the creation of a monetary union from the outset.

The CFA Franc Zone

The CFA franc zone[3] was established in 1948 by 14 countries in West and Central Africa to provide an anchor for their economic and financial policies. The two groupings of sub-Saharan countries, the WAEMU and the CAEMC, each has its own central bank—the Banque Centrale des États de l'Afrique de l'Ouest (BCEAO) and the Banque des États de l'Afrique Centrale (BEAC), respectively.[4] Each central bank has an operations account with the French Treasury, into which 65 percent of their foreign exchange holdings are deposited. The regime resembles a currency board type of arrangement, with the CFA franc fixed exchange rate—only changed once since 1948 (see below). Convertibility is guaranteed by provisions for overdrafts at the French Treasury and by a requirement that a percentage of local monetary liabilities be backed by foreign reserves deposited at the French Treasury. The central banks are required by their statutes to maintain 20 percent foreign exchange coverage of their sight liabilities, a limit designed to act as a barrier against open-ended access to the operations accounts that the central banks maintain with the French Treasury.

The countries of the CFA franc zone experienced from the beginning a long period of very low inflation, and, until the mid-1980s, sustained economic growth. During the second half of the 1980s and in the early 1990s, however, these countries faced two major external shocks that adversely affected their growth performance and balance of payments positions. First, the zone's terms of trade deteriorated by about 50 percent during the second half of the 1980s as the world market prices for its major export commodities—cocoa, coffee, cotton, and petroleum—

By Rina Bhattacharya and Andrea Schaechter.

[1]Bordo and Jonung (1999) analyze the establishment of monetary unions in the late eighteenth and nineteenth centuries.

[2]In 2000, the leaders of six West African non-CFA zone countries declared their intention to form a monetary union by 2003, as a first step toward creating a wider monetary union, including all 15 member countries of the Economic Community of West African States (ECOWAS), of which eight are already members of the WAEMU.

[3]IMF studies on the CFA franc zone include Clément and others (1996), Hernández-Catá and others (1998), and Masson and Pattillo (2001).

[4]At present, the eight members of WAEMU are Benin, Burkina Faso, Côte d'Ivoire, Guinea-Bissau, Mali, Niger, Senegal, and Togo. The six member countries of CAEMC are Cameroon, the Central African Republic, Chad, the Republic of Congo, Equatorial Guinea, and Gabon.

dropped sharply. At the same time, the external competitiveness of the zone deteriorated further as a result of the marked appreciation of the French franc against the currencies of the zone's other major trading partners. Combined with labor market rigidities that led to a steep rise in unit labor costs, the result was a considerable real effective exchange rate appreciation of the CFA franc that contributed to a stagnation of real output from 1986 onward.

This deteriorating economic situation was aggravated by indirect bank financing of government spending. Although central bank financing to each member country was subject to a limit equal to 20 percent of their previous year's budgetary revenues, credits for marketing and stockpiling of crop exports were excluded from this limit. Throughout the 1980s and early 1990s, this type of financing constituted a source of monetary expansion outside the BEAC's control. These credits were rediscounted automatically and at concessional rates. A similar situation existed in the West African CFA franc countries. Côte d'Ivoire and Senegal were able to avoid direct controls on financing by borrowing from commercial and development banks, which could obtain refinancing from the BCEAO at concessional rates. The lack of control over these credits opened the door to excessive lending to governments, despite the formal acknowledgement of the ceilings on direct financing. The result was large and growing fiscal deficits in CFA franc countries that exacerbated the overvaluation of the CFA franc. In addition, since prudential ratios on banks were not adequately enforced, banking crises occurred in CFA franc countries in the late 1980s and early 1990s, and the central banks—which had extended loans to the commercial and development banks—ended up as the major creditors. In January 1994, the 14 countries of the CFA franc zone ceased to rely exclusively on measures of internal adjustment and decided collectively to devalue their common currency by 50 percent. This exchange rate realignment led to a significant turnaround in economic activity in the zone, with output, exports, and investment increasing rapidly during the second half of the 1990s, while there was little inflation pass-through.

Although the CFA franc countries have had a monetary union for several decades, full economic integration has only progressed gradually. In 1973, the West African Economic Community (WAEC) was founded in response to the drawbacks of a previous customs union that attempted unsuccessfully to create a preferential internal regime in the absence of a common external tariff. The WAEC created a more adequate instrument of compensation for lost tariff revenues through a regional tax. In 1994, WAEC was superseded by the WAEMU, which established an economic and monetary union and has since put in place a common external tariff, introduced fiscal convergence criteria, and established a degree of surveillance over fiscal policies. WAEMU's budgetary convergence criteria are assessed through the concept of basic fiscal central government balance—defined as fiscal revenue minus expenditures and excluding both grants and foreign-financed investment. This balance has to be positive or nil. Moreover, a ceiling of 70 percent was set up for the overall ratio of public debt to GDP. The convergence pact has also restricted the sources of budget financing to public debt issues; thus, eliminating arrears and monetary financing by the regional central banks.

By contrast, regional integration has been slower in Central African CFA countries. The treaty creating CAEMC, signed in 1994, was only ratified in June 1999. In fact, their first mutual surveillance exercises using new fiscal and other criteria took place in 2002. With oil receipts being an important source of fiscal revenue in several CAEMC countries, fiscal convergence has been difficult to gauge in times of volatile oil prices. One alternative being currently considered is to use moving average of oil prices to better gauge the underlying fiscal position, as well as set up oil funds for future generations to take some of that revenue out of the budget to increase total savings. Moreover, although reforms pushed by its predecessor organization were in principle achieved (creating a common external tariff and a preferential internal tariff and the harmonization of indirect and business taxes), in practice, they have been unevenly applied.

Eastern Caribbean Currency Union

The ECCU[5] comprises eight small island economies: Anguilla, Antigua and Barbuda, Dominica, Grenada, Montserrat, St. Kitts and Nevis, St. Lucia, and St. Vincent and the Grenadines. The economies have traditionally been primary commodity producers (banana, sugar, root crops), but tourism is now the most important source of foreign exchange earnings. Two aspects of the ECCU members stand out: their very small size, and their vulnerability to shocks. Geographic barriers complicate the functioning of a single market, and even taken as a whole, the ECCU is a very small economy.[6] The individual economies are exposed to natural disasters—particularly hurricanes, and less frequently drought and volcanic eruption.

---

[5]For a more detailed analysis of the ECCU, see van Beek and others (2000).

[6]The ECCU had a total population of approximately half a million and a combined GDP of less than $3 billion in 2001.

The East Caribbean Currency Authority was formed in 1965 as the monetary authority for ECCU members and replaced in 1983 by the Eastern Caribbean Central Bank (ECCB). The members share a common currency, the Eastern Caribbean dollar, which has been pegged to the U.S. dollar since 1976, and was formerly pegged to the British pound. There is a single central bank for the monetary union and a single monetary policy. The ECCB operates as a quasi currency board, in which lending to member governments is strictly limited by statute, and 60 percent of its monetary liabilities are required to be backed by foreign currency assets. Foreign assets are part of a common pool and are not assigned to individual members. The main objective of monetary policy is to maintain foreign exchange cover.

Under the institutional arrangement described above, there is clearly no possibility for an independent monetary policy at the national level. The trend rate of inflation in the region is determined fundamentally by inflation in the United States and the other main trading partners, while market interest rates within the region follow U.S. interest rates closely with a premium reflecting local conditions. Restrictions on capital flows have in the past impeded the creation of a single money market and contributed to the segmentation of the regional banking market and the persistence of large spreads between lending and deposit rates, as well as differences in rates across economies. However, the region's trading systems are relatively open.

The ECCU and the ECCB provide an impressive example of successful, long-standing monetary cooperation. The monetary and exchange rate arrangements maintained by the union have been instrumental in facilitating domestic price and exchange rate stability. Despite the relatively frequent occurrence of major natural disasters, and the secular decline of key economic activities, the financial systems in the region have remained stable and virtually free from banking crises. A primary factor behind the success of the monetary union has been the strong Eastern Caribbean dollar policy pursued by the ECCB, which has imposed hard limits on its ability to extend credit to participating governments. Indeed, the ECCB has maintained foreign exchange backing of around 95 percent of monetary liabilities, well in excess of the minimum requirement of 60 percent set in the 1983 Act of Agreement. This has been possible because this act stipulates that lending to governments, up to prescribed limits, is at the discretion of the ECCB, and because member governments have exercised restraint in borrowing from the common central bank.

Each member conducts fiscal policy in the region independently. In sharp contrast to the recent experience with the EMU, there have been no fiscal harmonization criteria or targets, though the common currency arrangement has fostered a tradition of fiscal discipline across members. However, there have been exceptions, with some economies recording at times sizable fiscal deficits (financed without recourse to ECCB credit) by borrowing from external or domestic creditors. Moreover, in several economies in the region, public sector savings have been low in recent years, sometimes with adverse consequences for public investment and growth of output and employment.

Monetary union among these Caribbean economies has not stimulated significant development of intraregional trade despite trade liberalization. Trade was liberalized with the implementation of the common external tariff (CET) under the CARICOM agreement of 1992, which committed the signatories to reduce import tariffs to a maximum of 20 percent over six years starting in 1993. All economies in the region reduced the maximum tariff to 35 percent in 1993, but since then progress in this area has proceeded at differing paces, with St. Vincent and the Grenadines adhering strictly to the timetable for phased reductions and Antigua and Barbuda, as well as St. Kitts and Nevis and Anguilla lagging the most. Their slow progress has been related mostly to concerns about the effect of tariff reductions on government revenues and on certain domestic activities. Moreover, nontariff barriers are widespread in the region. In particular, import licenses are widely used, since Article 56 of the CARICOM Agreement allows protection of domestic production from competition by more advanced CARICOM members. In addition, members maintain licensing requirements to import a broad range of products from outside CARICOM. For these and other reasons the share of intraregional trade in total trade is relatively low. Although complete data are not available, rough estimates based on the IMF's *Direction of Trade Statistics* suggest that less than 10 percent of ECCU members' total trade is accounted for by trade within the region.

European Economic and Monetary Union

The euro area came into effect on January 1, 1999, and currently comprises 12 countries.[7] In contrast to the other monetary unions—which first established a monetary union before engaging in efforts to strengthen economic and financial integration—the

---

[7]Austria, Belgium, Finland, France, Germany, Greece (joined in 2001), Ireland, Italy, Luxembourg, the Netherlands, Portugal, and Spain. The history of the Economic and Monetary Union is described in detail on the ECB website (http://www.ecb. int). For a detailed description of the monetary policy strategy and policy instruments, see ECB (2001d).

EMU followed a long transition period, and the prior creation of a customs union in 1957, and of a single market for goods and factors in 1986. The Werner Report of 1970 recommended a monetary union among the then European Community members by 1980, but it was not until June 1988 that the European Union (EU) heads of government invited the then President of the European Commission, Jacques Delors, to produce a report on an economic and monetary union.

Following the 1989 Delors Committee Report, the EMU was established in three stages. The first stage (from July 1, 1990) abolished capital controls and involved coordination of national monetary policies and fostering of economic convergence. The first phase also saw the signing of the Maastricht Treaty (December 1991), which laid out the commitments underpinning the single currency. The Treaty mandated a long transition period, in which countries had to prove that they had converged to low fiscal deficits, inflation, and interest rates, manageable government debt, and exchange rate stability. Nevertheless, the road to a monetary union was not smooth. The Danes rejected the Treaty at a referendum in June 1992, and the United Kingdom negotiated the right to stay out of the single currency at its inception, though choose to join at a later stage. The monetary union faced a further setback with the speculative attacks against a number of European Monetary System (EMS) currencies from September 1992 to July 1993, the subsequent withdrawal of the Italian lira and pound sterling from the exchange rate mechanism, and devaluations of several other central parities.

In stage two (from January 1, 1994), the European Monetary Institute was set up as a precursor to the European Central Bank (ECB). At the time when the ECB was established in June 1998, also the bilateral conversion rates were announced. Moreover, stage two was characterized by economic convergence to fulfill the Maastricht criteria. The third and final stage of monetary union took place on January 1, 1999, with the launching of the euro—when the rates of conversion between the euro and 11 European currencies were irrevocably fixed (Greece joined the EMU in 2001). On January 1, 2002, euro notes and coins were introduced, with the agreement that all previous national notes and coins were to be withdrawn from circulation no later than July 2002.

At the onset of the EMU, intraregional trade already accounted for a significant share of total trade unlike most of the other monetary unions (internal trade within the EU was 46 percent of both imports and exports of member countries in the late 1990s). Economic activity in the countries of the euro area is fairly integrated, with individual country's production being relatively similar and diversified. Since the transition period to EMU, the EMU economies have converged in many aspects. Inflation has come down, budget deficits are smaller, and the level of government debt has also fallen. The introduction of the euro has also increased price transparency and competition in the marketplace, lowered transaction costs, and enhanced greater financing and investment opportunities in the deeper and more liquid euro-denominated financial markets.

Together the ECB and the national central banks make up the European System of Central Banks (ESCB). Monetary policy is determined by the ECB, though implemented in part by the national central banks. There is a single monetary policy and set of official central bank interest rates for the entire zone. Foreign exchange reserves are partly pooled and partly retained by national central banks. The two main decision-making bodies of the ECB are the Executive Board and the Governing Council. The main task of the Executive Board (consisting of the ECB's President, Vice-President and four other members) is to implement monetary policy in accordance with the guidelines and decisions laid down by the Governing Council by giving instructions to the national central banks. The Governing Council, which is responsible for formulating the single monetary policy and setting guidelines for its implementation, comprises the Executive Board and the governors of the national central banks of the 12 euro area countries.[8]

The main objective of monetary policy is to maintain price stability, and subject to that objective being achieved, to support economic activity. The ECB's Governing Council has stated that in the pursuit of price stability, it will aim to maintain inflation rates close to 2 percent over the medium term, providing a sufficient margin to guard against the risk of deflation. It has also indicated that the ECB will not respond to short-run deviations from the inflation objective arising from shocks to energy prices or other sources. The ECB has formulated a two-pillar strategy to achieve this inflation objective. The first pillar assigns a prominent role to the growth rate of M3 for which it has set a reference growth value of 4.5 percent. The second pillar is a broadly based assessment of the outlook of price developments and risks to price stability in the euro area as a whole using a wide range of economic and financial indicator variables, such as long-term in-

---

[8]Currently each euro member has one vote, and most decisions—including those on monetary policy—can be taken by simple majority. However, votes for decisions that affect the positions of the national central banks as shareholders of the ESCB (e.g., relating to the capital and the foreign exchange reserves of the ECB) are weighted by the share of each national central bank in the ECB's capital.

terest rates and the yield curve, as well as indicators of consumer and business confidence, wages and unit labor costs, and others.

The ECB has a range of instruments at its disposal for implementing monetary policy. Open market operations are used to manage liquidity in the money market and to steer short-term interest rates. The most important instrument is reverse transactions (applicable on the basis of repurchase agreements or collateralized loans). They are initiated by the ECB, but are normally carried out through the national central banks. In addition, two standing facilities—the marginal lending and deposit facilities—allow eligible counterparties to cover their overnight liquidity needs or to invest their daily liquidity surpluses. The marginal lending rate normally determines the ceiling for the overnight market interest rate while the deposit rate normally represents the floor. Credit institutions are also required to hold a minimum of 2 percent of specified liabilities as reserves on their account with the national central banks. These required reserves are remunerated at a level corresponding to the weekly tender rate for the main reverse operations, broadly in line with market conditions.

The Treaty strictly prohibits direct or indirect monetary financing of governments. Moreover, the constraints on fiscal policy upon joining the monetary union were further strengthened by agreeing on the Stability and Growth Pact. The member states have committed themselves to respect the medium-term budgetary objective of positions close to balance or in surplus. Deficits of 3 percent of GDP are regarded as excessive, unless they are expected to be temporary and have occurred under exceptional circumstances. The Stability and Growth Pact also defines those circumstances and lays out the process for implementing the excessive deficit procedure that can ultimately result in sanctions of up to half a percent of GDP.[9] These fines are not automatic and require majority approval among the EU members, and they are not paid for at least two years. Portugal and Germany have been the first countries for which the Council decided that excessive deficits existed. Those instances have fueled anew the discussion about the role of the Pact, its design, and effectiveness. Some have argued to relax the Pact because it has left the members without sufficient flexibility in times of economic slowdown. Suggestions include relaxing the tight definitions for exceptional circumstances, focusing on cyclically adjusted deficits, and being less strict with countries that have lower levels of debt. Nevertheless, there is general agreement that rules and procedures to ensure fiscal prudence in EMU are crucial to avoid negative externalities, even though there might be room to revise some aspects of the existing fiscal rules in the future.

Some concerns have been expressed regarding the institutional setup of the EMU. One is that the monetary policy institutional framework lacks a central lender of last resort. The ECB has not been granted power by the Treaty to serve this function, in sharp contrast with other modern central banks, that exercise lender-of-last-resort responsibilities to guarantee the liquidity and functioning of the payments system. In addition, there is no central authority to supervise the financial systems, including the commercial banks, operating in the euro area. The Maastricht Treaty gives the ECB some supervisory functions, but they are primarily the task of the union member countries. To address these issues, a Memorandum of Understanding has been signed that lays out some key principles of cooperation between the banking supervisors and central banks of the EU in crisis management situations.

---

[9]The Stability and Growth Pact and its implementation process is described in ECB (1999a).

Bibliography

Abed, George T., S. Nuri Erbas, and Behrouz Guerami, 2003, "The GCC Monetary Union: Some Considerations for the Exchange Rate Regime," IMF Working Paper No. 03/66 (Washington: International Monetary Fund).

Alexander, William E., Tomás J.T. Baliño, and Charles Enoch, 1995, *The Adoption of Indirect Instruments of Monetary Policy*, IMF Occasional Paper No. 126 (Washington: International Monetary Fund).

Alesina, Alberto, and Robert J. Barro, eds., 2001, *Currency Unions* (Stanford, California: Hoover Institution Press, Stanford University).

Allen, Polly Reynolds, 1976, *Organization and Administration of a Monetary Union*, Princeton Studies in International Finance No. 38 (Princeton, New Jersey: Princeton University Press).

Askari, Hossein, Vahid Nowshirvani, and Mohamed Jaber, 1997, *Economic Development in the GCC: The Blessing and the Curse of Oil* (Greenwich, Connecticut: JAI Press).

Barnett, Steven A., and Rolando J. Ossowski, 2002, "Operational Aspects of Fiscal Policy in Oil-Producing Countries," IMF Working Paper No. 02/177 (Washington: International Monetary Fund).

Bayoumi, Tamim, and Barry Eichengreen, 1994, *One Money or Many? Analyzing the Prospects for Monetary Unification in Various Parts of the World,* Princeton Studies in International Finance No. 76 (Princeton, New Jersey: Princeton University Press).

Beetsma, Roel, Xavier Debrun, and Franc Klaassen, 2001, "Is Fiscal Policy Coordination in EMU Desirable?" IMF Working Paper No. 01/178 (Washington: International Monetary Fund).

Blejer, Mario I., Jacob A. Frenkel, Leonardo Leiderman, and Assaf Razin, eds., 1997, *Optimum Currency Areas, New Analytical and Policy Developments* (Washington: International Monetary Fund).

Bordo, Michael D., and Lars Jonung, 1999, "The Future of EMU: What Does the History of Monetary Unions Tell Us?" NBER Working Paper No. 7365 (Cambridge, Massachusetts: National Bureau of Economic Research).

Clément, Jean A.P., and others, 1996, *Aftermath of the CFA Franc Devaluation*, IMF Occasional Paper No. 138 (Washington: International Monetary Fund).

Davis, Jeffrey, Rolando Ossowski, James Daniel, and Steven Barnett, 2001, *Stabilization and Savings Funds for Nonrenewable Resources: Experience and Fiscal Policy Implications*, IMF Occasional Paper No. 205 (Washington: International Monetary Fund).

De Grauwe, Paul, and Wim Vanhaverbeke, 1991, "Is Europe an Optimum Currency Area? Evidence From Regional Data," CEPR Discussion Paper No. 555 (London: Centre for Economic Policy Research).

de la Torre, Augusto, and Kelly, Margaret R., 1992, *Regional Trade Arrangements*, IMF Occasional Paper No. 93 (Washington: International Monetary Fund).

Doré, Ousmane, and Paul R. Masson, 2002 "Experience with Budgetary Convergence in the WAEMU," IMF Working Paper No. 02/108 (Washington: International Monetary Fund).

Deutsche Bundesbank, 2000, "The Integration of the German Money Market in the Single Euro Money Market," in Monthly Report January 2000, pp.15–30 (Frankfurt).

Eichengreen, Barry, 1997, "Is Europe an Optimum Currency Area?" in *European Monetary Unification: Theory, Practice, and Analysis,* by Barry Eichengreen (Cambridge, Massachusetts: MIT Press).

El-Erian, Mohamed A., and Stanley Fischer, 1996, "Is MENA a Region? The Scope for Regional Integration," IMF Working Paper No. 96/30 (Washington: International Monetary Fund).

Engel, Eduardo, and Rodrigo O. Valdes, 2000, "Optimal Fiscal Strategy for Oil Exporting Countries," IMF Working Paper No. 00/118 (Washington: International Monetary Fund).

European Central Bank, 1999a, "Banking in the Euro Area: Structural Features and Trends," *Monthly Report* (April), pp. 41–53.

———, 1999b, "The Implementation of the Stability and Growth Pact," *Monthly Report* (May), pp. 45–72.

———, 2000, "EMU and Banking Supervision," *Monthly Bulletin* (April), pp. 49–64.

———, 2001a, *The Euro Money Market,* July (Frankfurt).

———, 2001b, *The Euro Bond Market,* July (Frankfurt).

———, 2001c, *The Euro Equity Markets*, August (Frankfurt).

———, 2001d, *The Monetary Policy of the ECB* (Frankfurt).

European Commission, 1990, "One Market, One Money: An Evaluation of the Potential Benefits and Costs of Forming An Economic and Monetary Union," *European Economy*, Vol. 44.

———, 1996, *Credit Institutions and Banking*, The Single Market Review Series. Subseries II—Impact on Services (Brussels).

————, 1999, Report of the Giovannini Group, *EU Repo Markets: Opportunities for Change* (Brussels).

————, Economic and Financial Committee, 2001, *Report on Financial Crisis Management*, EFC/ECFIN/251/01 (Brussels).

Fasano, Ugo, 2000, "Review of the Experience with Oil Stabilization and Savings Funds in Selected Countries," IMF Working Paper No. 00/112 (Washington: International Monetary Fund).

————, 2001a, "With Limited Oil Resources, Oman Faces Challenges of Economic Diversification, Structural Reforms," *IMF Survey,* Vol., 30, No. 15 (July 30), pp. 254–57.

————, 2001b, "Sluggish Growth, Declining Oil Resources Prompt Qatar to Diversify Economy Away from Oil" *IMF Survey,* Vol, 30, No. 22 (November 26), pp. 382–84.

————, 2002, "With Open Economy and Sound Policies, U.A.E. Has Turned Oil 'Curse' into a Blessing," *IMF Survey,* Vol. 31, No. 19 (October 21), pp. 330–32.

————, 2003, "Fiscal Sustainability with Oil Resources," in *United Arab Emirates: Selected Issues and Statistical Appendix*, IMF Country Report No. 03/67 (Washington: International Monetary Fund), pp. 38–41.

Fasano, Ugo, and Zubair Iqbal, 2002, "Common Currency," *Finance & Development*, Vol. 39 (December), pp. 42–45.

Fasano, Ugo, and Qing Wang, 2001, "Fiscal Expenditure Policy and Non-Oil Economic Growth: Evidence from GCC Countries," IMF Working Paper No. 01/195 (Washington: International Monetary Fund).

————, 2002, "Testing the Relationship Between Government Spending and Revenue: Evidence from GCC Countries," IMF Working Paper No. 02/201 (Washington: International Monetary Fund).

Fasano, Ugo, and Rishi Goyal, 2003, "Rising Unemployment in GCC Countries: Policy Options," forthcoming IMF Working Paper.

Hernández-Catá, Ernesto, and others, 1998, *The West African Economic and Monetary Union*, IMF Occasional Paper No. 170 (Washington: International Monetary Fund).

International Monetary Fund, 2003, "United Arab Emirates: Financial System Stability Assessment, Including Reports on the Observance of Standards and Codes on the Following Topics: Monetary and Financial Policy Transparency, Banking Supervision and Payment Systems," IMF Country Report No. 03/20 (Washington).

Issing, Otmar, 1999, "The Monetary Policy of the Eurosystem," *Finance & Development*, Vol. 36 (March), pp. 18–21.

Jadresic, Esteban, 2002, "On a Common Currency for the GCC Countries," IMF Policy Discussion Paper No. 02/12 (Washington: International Monetary Fund).

Jahjah, Samir, 2001, "Financial Stability and Fiscal Crises in a Monetary Union," IMF Working Paper No. 01/201 (Washington: International Monetary Fund).

Kopits, George, ed., 1992, *Tax Harmonization in the European Community: Policy Issues and Analysis*, IMF Occasional Paper No. 94 (Washington: International Monetary Fund).

Masson, Paul, and Jacques Mélitz, 1991, "Fiscal Policy Independence in a European Monetary Union," *Open Economics Review*, Vol. 2, pp. 113–36.

Masson, Paul, and Catherine Pattillo, 2001, *Monetary Union in West Africa (ECOWAS): Is It Desirable and How Could It Be Achieved?*, IMF Occasional Paper No. 204 (Washington: International Monetary Fund).

Masson, Paul, and Mark Taylor, 1993, "Currency Unions: A Survey of the Issues," in *Policy Issues in the Operation of Currency Unions*, ed. by Paul Masson and Mark Taylor (Cambridge and New York: Cambridge University Press).

Mélitz, Jacques, and Axel A. Weber, 1996, "The Costs/Benefits of a Common Monetary Policy in France and Germany and Possible Lessons for Monetary Union," CEPR Discussion Paper No. 1374 (London: Centre for Economic Policy Research).

Mehran, Hassanali, and others, 1998, *Financial Sector Development in Sub-Saharan African Countries*, IMF Occasional Paper No. 169 (Washington: International Monetary Fund).

Mundell, Robert A., 1961, "A Theory of Optimum Currency Areas," *American Economic Review*, Vol. 51, pp. 657–64.

————, 1997, "Updating the Agenda for Monetary Union," in *Optimum Currency Areas: New Analytical and Policy Developments*, ed. by Mario Blejer, Jacob A. Frenkel, Leonardo Leiderman, and Assaf Razin (Washington: International Monetary Fund).

Padoa-Schioppa, Tommaso, 1994, *The Road to Monetary Union in Europe: The Emperor, the Kings, and the Genies* (Oxford: Clarendon Press).

————, 1999, "EMU and Banking Supervision," lecture delivered at the London School of Economics, Financial Markets Group, February 24.

————, 2000, "The Eurosystem and Financial Stability," speech delivered at the Belgian Financial Forum, February 10.

Persson, Torsten, 2001, "Currency Unions and Trade: How Large Is the Treatment Effect?" *Economic Policy: A European Forum*, No. 33 (October) pp. 435–61.

Rose, Andrew, 2000, "One Money, One Market: Estimating the Effects of Common Currencies on Trade," *Economic Policy: A European Forum*, No. 30 (April) pp. 9–45.

Sandwick, John A., ed., 1987, *The Gulf Cooperation Council: Moderation and Stability in an Interdependent World* (Boulder, Colorado: Westview Press).

Santillán, Javier, Marc Bayle, and Christian Thygesen, 2000, *The Impact of the Euro on Money and Bond Markets*, ECB Occasional Paper No. 1 (Frankfurt: European Central Bank).

Sinn, Hans-Werner, and Holger Feist, 1997, "Eurowinners and Eurolosers: The Distribution of Seigniorage Wealth in EMU," NBER Working Paper No. 6072 (Cambridge, Massachusetts: National Bureau of Economic Research).

Tenreyro, Silvana 2001, "On the Causes and Consequences of Currency Unions," paper presented at an IMF Research Department Seminar, December 5.

van Beek, Frits, José Roberto Rosales, Mayra Zermeño, Ruby Randall, and Jorge Shepherd, 2000, *The East-*

ern Caribbean Currency Union: Institutions, Performance, and Policy Issues, IMF Occasional Paper No. 195 (Washington: International Monetary Fund).

Williams, Oral, Tracy Polius, and Selvon Hazel, 2001, "Reserve Pooling in the Eastern Caribbean Currency Union and the CFA Franc Zone: A Comparative Analysis," IMF Working Paper No. 01/104 (Washington: International Monetary Fund).

World Bank, 2001, *World Development Indicators* (Washington).

Recent Occasional Papers of the International Monetary Fund

223. Monetary Union Among Member Countries of the Gulf Cooperation Council, by a staff team led by Ugo Fasano. 2003.

222. Informal Funds Transfer Systems: An Analysis of the Informal Hawala System, by Mohammed El Qorchi, Samuel Munzele Maimbo, and John F. Wilson. 2003.

221. Deflation: Determinants, Risks, and Policy Options, by Manmohan S. Kumar. 2003.

220. Effects of Financial Globalization on Developing Countries: Some Empirical Evidence, by Eswar S. Prasad, Kenneth Rogoff, Shang-Jin Wei, and Ayhan Kose. 2003.

219. Economic Policy in a Highly Dollarized Economy: The Case of Cambodia, by Mario de Zamaroczy and Sopanha Sa. 2003.

218. Fiscal Vulnerability and Financial Crises in Emerging Market Economies, by Richard Hemming, Michael Kell, and Axel Schimmelpfennig. 2003.

217. Managing Financial Crises: Recent Experience and Lessons for Latin America, edited by Charles Collyns and G. Russell Kincaid. 2003.

216. Is the PRGF Living Up to Expectations?—An Assessment of Program Design, by Sanjeev Gupta, Mark Plant, Benedict Clements, Thomas Dorsey, Emanuele Baldacci, Gabriela Inchauste, Shamsuddin Tareq, and Nita Thacker. 2002.

215. Improving Large Taxpayers' Compliance: A Review of Country Experience, by Katherine Baer. 2002.

214. Advanced Country Experiences with Capital Account Liberalization, by Age Bakker and Bryan Chapple. 2002.

213. The Baltic Countries: Medium-Term Fiscal Issues Related to EU and NATO Accession, by Johannes Mueller, Christian Beddies, Robert Burgess, Vitali Kramarenko, and Joannes Mongardini. 2002.

212. Financial Soundness Indicators: Analytical Aspects and Country Practices, by V. Sundararajan, Charles Enoch, Armida San José, Paul Hilbers, Russell Krueger, Marina Moretti, and Graham Slack. 2002.

211. Capital Account Liberalization and Financial Sector Stability, by a staff team led by Shogo Ishii and Karl Habermeier. 2002.

210. IMF-Supported Programs in Capital Account Crises, by Atish Ghosh, Timothy Lane, Marianne Schulze-Ghattas, Aleš Bulíř, Javier Hamann, and Alex Mourmouras. 2002.

209. Methodology for Current Account and Exchange Rate Assessments, by Peter Isard, Hamid Faruqee, G. Russell Kincaid, and Martin Fetherston. 2001.

208. Yemen in the 1990s: From Unification to Economic Reform, by Klaus Enders, Sherwyn Williams, Nada Choueiri, Yuri Sobolev, and Jan Walliser. 2001.

207. Malaysia: From Crisis to Recovery, by Kanitta Meesook, Il Houng Lee, Olin Liu, Yougesh Khatri, Natalia Tamirisa, Michael Moore, and Mark H. Krysl. 2001.

206. The Dominican Republic: Stabilization, Structural Reform, and Economic Growth, by Alessandro Giustiniani, Werner C. Keller, and Randa E. Sab. 2001.

205. Stabilization and Savings Funds for Nonrenewable Resources, by Jeffrey Davis, Rolando Ossowski, James Daniel, and Steven Barnett. 2001.

204. Monetary Union in West Africa (ECOWAS): Is It Desirable and How Could It Be Achieved? by Paul Masson and Catherine Pattillo. 2001.

203. Modern Banking and OTC Derivatives Markets: The Transformation of Global Finance and Its Implications for Systemic Risk, by Garry J. Schinasi, R. Sean Craig, Burkhard Drees, and Charles Kramer. 2000.

202. Adopting Inflation Targeting: Practical Issues for Emerging Market Countries, by Andrea Schaechter, Mark R. Stone, and Mark Zelmer. 2000.

201. Developments and Challenges in the Caribbean Region, by Samuel Itam, Simon Cueva, Erik Lundback, Janet Stotsky, and Stephen Tokarick. 2000.

200. Pension Reform in the Baltics: Issues and Prospects, by Jerald Schiff, Niko Hobdari, Axel Schimmelpfennig, and Roman Zytek. 2000.

199. Ghana: Economic Development in a Democratic Environment, by Sérgio Pereira Leite, Anthony Pel-lechio, Luisa Zanforlin, Girma Begashaw, Stefania Fabrizio, and Joachim Harnack. 2000.

198. Setting Up Treasuries in the Baltics, Russia, and Other Countries of the Former Soviet Union: An Assess-ment of IMF Technical Assistance, by Barry H. Potter and Jack Diamond. 2000.

197. Deposit Insurance: Actual and Good Practices, by Gillian G.H. Garcia. 2000.

196. Trade and Trade Policies in Eastern and Southern Africa, by a staff team led by Arvind Subramanian, with Enrique Gelbard, Richard Harmsen, Katrin Elborgh-Woytek, and Piroska Nagy. 2000.

195. The Eastern Caribbean Currency Union—Institutions, Performance, and Policy Issues, by Frits van Beek, José Roberto Rosales, Mayra Zermeño, Ruby Randall, and Jorge Shepherd. 2000.

194. Fiscal and Macroeconomic Impact of Privatization, by Jeffrey Davis, Rolando Ossowski, Thomas Richardson, and Steven Barnett. 2000.

193. Exchange Rate Regimes in an Increasingly Integrated World Economy, by Michael Mussa, Paul Masson, Alexander Swoboda, Esteban Jadresic, Paolo Mauro, and Andy Berg. 2000.

192. Macroprudential Indicators of Financial System Soundness, by a staff team led by Owen Evans, Alfredo M. Leone, Mahinder Gill, and Paul Hilbers. 2000.

191. Social Issues in IMF-Supported Programs, by Sanjeev Gupta, Louis Dicks-Mireaux, Ritha Khemani, Calvin McDonald, and Marijn Verhoeven. 2000.

190. Capital Controls: Country Experiences with Their Use and Liberalization, by Akira Ariyoshi, Karl Haber-meier, Bernard Laurens, Inci Ötker-Robe, Jorge Iván Canales Kriljenko, and Andrei Kirilenko. 2000.

189. Current Account and External Sustainability in the Baltics, Russia, and Other Countries of the Former Soviet Union, by Donal McGettigan. 2000.

188. Financial Sector Crisis and Restructuring: Lessons from Asia, by Carl-Johan Lindgren, Tomás J.T. Baliño, Charles Enoch, Anne-Marie Gulde, Marc Quintyn, and Leslie Teo. 1999.

187. Philippines: Toward Sustainable and Rapid Growth, Recent Developments and the Agenda Ahead, by Markus Rodlauer, Prakash Loungani, Vivek Arora, Charalambos Christofides, Enrique G. De la Piedra, Piyabha Kongsamut, Kristina Kostial, Victoria Summers, and Athanasios Vamvakidis. 2000.

186. Anticipating Balance of Payments Crises: The Role of Early Warning Systems, by Andrew Berg, Eduardo Borensztein, Gian Maria Milesi-Ferretti, and Catherine Pattillo. 1999.

185. Oman Beyond the Oil Horizon: Policies Toward Sustainable Growth, edited by Ahsan Mansur and Volker Treichel. 1999.

184. Growth Experience in Transition Countries, 1990–98, by Oleh Havrylyshyn, Thomas Wolf, Julian Beren-gaut, Marta Castello-Branco, Ron van Rooden, and Valerie Mercer-Blackman. 1999.

183. Economic Reforms in Kazakhstan, Kyrgyz Republic, Tajikistan, Turkmenistan, and Uzbekistan, by Emine Gürgen, Harry Snoek, Jon Craig, Jimmy McHugh, Ivailo Izvorski, and Ron van Rooden. 1999.

182. Tax Reform in the Baltics, Russia, and Other Countries of the Former Soviet Union, by a staff team led by Liam Ebrill and Oleh Havrylyshyn. 1999.

181. The Netherlands: Transforming a Market Economy, by C. Maxwell Watson, Bas B. Bakker, Jan Kees Martijn, and Ioannis Halikias. 1999.

180. Revenue Implications of Trade Liberalization, by Liam Ebrill, Janet Stotsky, and Reint Gropp. 1999.

179. Disinflation in Transition: 1993–97, by Carlo Cottarelli and Peter Doyle. 1999.

178. IMF-Supported Programs in Indonesia, Korea, and Thailand: A Preliminary Assessment, by Timothy Lane, Atish Ghosh, Javier Hamann, Steven Phillips, Marianne Schulze-Ghattas, and Tsidi Tsikata. 1999.

177. Perspectives on Regional Unemployment in Europe, by Paolo Mauro, Eswar Prasad, and Antonio Spilim-bergo. 1999.

176. Back to the Future: Postwar Reconstruction and Stabilization in Lebanon, edited by Sena Eken and Thomas Helbling. 1999.

175. Macroeconomic Developments in the Baltics, Russia, and Other Countries of the Former Soviet Union, 1992–97, by Luis M. Valdivieso. 1998.

Note: For information on the titles and availability of Occasional Papers not listed, please consult the IMF's *Publications Catalog* or contact IMF Publication Services.